Just for Kids

Publications International, Ltd.

Microwave Cooking: Microwave ovens vary in wattage. Use the cooking times as guidelines and check for doneness before adding more time.

Preparation/Cooking Times: Preparation times are based on the approximate amount of time required to assemble the recipe before cooking, baking, chilling or serving. These times include preparation steps such as measuring, chopping and mixing. The fact that some preparations and cooking can be done simultaneously is taken into account. Preparation of optional ingredients and serving suggestions is not included.

Contents

86

146

158

Scrumptious Starters

Cheesy Quesadillas

Prep Time: 10 minutes   *Cook Time:* 15 minutes

½ pound ground beef
1 medium onion, chopped
¼ teaspoon salt
1 can (4.5 ounces) chopped green chilies, drained
1 jar (26 to 28 ounces) RAGÚ® Robusto!™ Pasta Sauce
8 (6½-inch) flour tortillas
1 tablespoon olive or vegetable oil
2 cups shredded Cheddar and/or mozzarella cheese (about 8 ounces)

1. Preheat oven to 400°F. In 12-inch skillet, brown ground beef with onion and salt over medium-high heat; drain. Stir in chilies and ½ cup Ragú Pasta Sauce; set aside.

2. Meanwhile, evenly brush one side of 4 tortillas with half of the oil. On cookie sheets, arrange tortillas, oil-side down. Evenly top with ½ of the cheese, beef filling, then remaining cheese. Top with remaining 4 tortillas, then brush tops with remaining oil.

3. Bake 10 minutes or until cheese is melted. To serve, cut each quesadilla into 4 wedges. Serve with remaining sauce, heated.

Makes 4 servings

Confetti Tuna in Celery Sticks

Prep Time: 20 minutes

1 (3-ounce) pouch of STARKIST® Premium Albacore or Chunk
    Light Tuna
½ cup shredded red or green cabbage
½ cup shredded carrot
¼ cup shredded yellow squash or zucchini
3 tablespoons reduced-calorie cream cheese, softened
1 tablespoon plain low-fat yogurt
½ teaspoon dried basil, crushed
    Salt and pepper to taste
10 to 12 (4-inch) celery sticks, with leaves if desired

1. In a small bowl toss together tuna, cabbage, carrot and squash.

2. Stir in cream cheese, yogurt and basil. Add salt and pepper to taste.

3. With small spatula spread mixture evenly into celery sticks.

Makes 10 to 12 servings

Sweet Nothings Trail Mix

Prep and Cook Time: 10 minutes

5 cups rice and corn cereal squares
1½ cups raisins
1½ cups small thin pretzel sticks, broken into pieces
1 cup candy-coated chocolate candy
1 cup peanuts

1. Have children decorate small resealable food storage bags with Valentine's Day stickers, if desired.

2. Combine cereal, raisins, pretzels, candy and peanuts in large resealable plastic food storage bag; shake well. Distribute evenly among decorated bags or serve in large bowl.

Makes 10 cups

Serve It With Style!: If you'd rather use this recipe as a party favor, wrap handfuls of trail mix in pink plastic wrap and tie with colored ribbons.

Caramel Apple Wedges

⅔ cup sugar
¼ cup butter, cut into small pieces
½ cup whipping cream
¼ teaspoon salt
 3 apples, cored and each apple cut into 6 wedges
½ cup shredded coconut
¼ cup mini chocolate chips

1. Place sugar in medium, heavy saucepan. Cook over low heat until sugar melts, about 20 minutes. Carefully stir in butter then cream. (Mixture will spatter.) Cook over low heat until any lumps disappear, about 15 minutes, stirring occasionally. Stir in salt.

2. To serve, pour caramel sauce into serving bowl or fondue pot over heat source. Arrange apple wedges on a plate. Combine coconut and chocolate chips in a separate serving dish.

3. Using fondue forks, dip apple wedges into caramel sauce, then into coconut mixture.

Makes 6 servings

Variation: To make caramel apples, combine 1 package (14 ounces) caramels and 2 tablespoons water in heavy saucepan. Melt over low heat, about 10 minutes. Roll apples in melted caramel mixture, then in coconut-chocolate chip mixture. Cool on sheet of waxed paper until firm.

Cheese Straws

½ cup (1 stick) butter, softened
⅛ teaspoon salt
    Dash ground red pepper
1 pound sharp Cheddar cheese, shredded, at room temperature
2 cups self-rising flour

Heat oven to 350°F. In mixer bowl, beat butter, salt and pepper until creamy. Add cheese; mix well. Gradually add flour, mixing until dough begins to form a ball. Form dough into ball with hands. Fit cookie press with small star plate; fill with dough according to manufacturer's directions. Press dough onto cookie sheets in 3-inch-long strips. Bake 12 minutes, just until lightly browned. Cool completely on wire rack. Store tightly covered.

Makes about 10 dozen

Favorite recipe from *Southeast United Dairy Industry Association, Inc.*

Quick Sand

¾ cup creamy peanut butter
 5 ounces cream cheese, softened
 1 jar (8 ounces or 1 cup) pineapple preserves
⅓ cup milk
 1 teaspoon Worcestershire sauce
   Dash hot pepper sauce (optional)
 1 can (7 ounces) refrigerated breadstick dough (6 breadsticks)
 5 rich round crackers, crushed
   Cut-up vegetables such as carrots and celery, or fruit such as
      apples and pears for dipping

1. Combine peanut butter and cream cheese in large bowl until well blended. Stir in preserves, milk, Worcestershire sauce and hot pepper sauce, if desired. Spread in 8- or 9-inch glass pie plate. Cover with plastic wrap and refrigerate until ready to serve.

2. Preheat oven to 375°F. Cut each breadstick in half crosswise; place on ungreased baking sheet. Make 3 slits in one short end of each breadstick half to resemble fingers. Cut small piece of dough from other short end; press dough piece into "hand" to resemble thumb. Bake 8 to 10 minutes or until golden brown.

3. Just before serving, sprinkle dip with cracker crumbs; serve with breadstick hands and vegetables and fruit. Garnish as desired.

Makes 12 to 16 servings

15

Cinnamon Trail Mix

2 cups corn cereal squares
2 cups whole wheat cereal squares or whole wheat cereal squares
    with mini graham crackers
1½ cups fat-free oyster crackers
½ cup broken sesame snack sticks
2 tablespoons margarine or butter, melted
1 teaspoon ground cinnamon
¼ teaspoon ground nutmeg
½ cup bite-sized fruit-flavored candy pieces

1. Preheat oven to 350°F. Spray 13×9-inch baking pan with nonstick cooking spray.

2. Place cereals, oyster crackers and sesame sticks in prepared pan; mix lightly.

3. Combine margarine, cinnamon and nutmeg in small bowl; mix well. Drizzle evenly over cereal mixture; toss to coat.

4. Bake 12 to 14 minutes or until golden brown, stirring gently after 6 minutes. Cool completely. Stir in candies.   *Makes 8 (¾-cup) servings*

Sugar-and-Spice Twists

1 tablespoon sugar
¼ teaspoon ground cinnamon
1 package (6) refrigerated breadsticks

Preheat oven to 350°F. Lightly grease baking sheet or line with parchment paper. Stir together sugar and cinnamon. Place on shallow dish or plate.

Open package of breadsticks. Divide into 6 portions. Roll each portion into 12-inch rope. Roll in sugar mixture. Twist into pretzel shape. Place on prepared baking sheet. Bake 15 to 18 minutes or until lightly browned. Remove from baking sheet. Cool 5 minutes. Serve warm.

Makes 6 servings

Cranberry Bog Gorp

¼ cup unsalted butter
¼ cup packed light brown sugar
1 tablespoon maple syrup
1 teaspoon curry powder
½ teaspoon ground cinnamon
1½ cups dried cranberries
1½ cups coarsely chopped walnuts and/or slivered almonds
1½ cups lightly salted pretzel nuggets

1. Preheat oven to 300°F. Melt butter, brown sugar and maple syrup in large saucepan over medium heat. Stir in curry powder and cinnamon. Add cranberries, walnuts and pretzels; stir to combine.

2. Spread mixture on greased 15×10-inch jelly-roll pan. Bake 15 minutes or until mixture is crunchy and lightly browned. *Makes 20 servings*

Fruity Gelatin Pops

Prep Time: 10 minutes   *Freezing Time:* 7 hours

1 cup boiling water
1 package (4-serving size) JELL-O® Brand Gelatin Dessert, any
    flavor
⅓ cup sugar
1⅓ cups cold juice, any flavor
6 (5-ounce) paper cups

STIR boiling water into gelatin and sugar in medium bowl at least
2 minutes until completely dissolved. Stir in cold juice. Pour into cups.
Freeze about 2 hours or until almost firm. Insert wooden pop stick into
each for handle.

FREEZE 5 hours or overnight until firm. To remove pop from cup, place
bottom of cup under warm running water for 15 seconds. Press firmly on
bottom of cup to release pop. (Do not twist or pull pop stick.) Store
leftover pops in freezer up to 2 weeks.   *Makes 6 pops*

Outrageous Orange Pops: Use 1 cup boiling water, JELL-O® Brand Orange
Flavor Gelatin Dessert, ⅓ cup sugar and 1⅓ cups orange juice.

Fruity Strawberry Pops: Use 1 cup boiling water, JELL-O® Brand
Strawberry Flavor Gelatin Dessert, ⅓ cup sugar, ⅔ cup cold water and
⅔ cup puréed strawberries.

Fizzy Grape Pops: Use 1 cup boiling water, JELL-O® Brand Sparkling White
Grape Flavor Gelatin Dessert, 2 tablespoons sugar and 1½ cups carbonated
grape beverage.

Lemonade Pops: Use 1 cup boiling water, JELL-O® Brand Lemon Flavor
Gelatin Dessert, ⅓ cup sugar, 1 cup cold water and 2 tablespoons lemon juice.

Iced Tea Pops: Use 1 cup boiling water, JELL-O® Brand Lemon Flavor
Gelatin Dessert, 2 tablespoons sugar and 1½ cups pre-sweetened iced tea.

Granola Crisp Topping with Fruit

⅓ cup old-fashioned rolled oats, uncooked
3 tablespoons chopped walnuts
¼ cup honey
1 egg white
¼ teaspoon vanilla
¼ teaspoon ground cinnamon
  Dash salt
2 cups nonfat plain or vanilla yogurt
2 cups mixed berries

Combine oats and walnuts in medium bowl. Mix together honey, egg white, vanilla, cinnamon and salt in small bowl until well blended. Add honey mixture to oats; stir until well blended. Line 11×17-inch baking sheet with foil; spray with nonstick cooking spray. Spread oat mixture in even layer on prepared baking sheet. Bake at 325°F 15 to 17 minutes or until golden brown, tossing mixture 3 to 4 times during baking. Remove from oven. Cool completely until crisp and crunchy. Serve over yogurt and berries.

Makes 4 servings

Favorite recipe from **National Honey Board**

Easy Nachos

4 (6-inch) flour tortillas
   Nonstick cooking spray
4 ounces ground turkey
⅔ cup salsa (mild or medium)
2 tablespoons sliced green onion
½ cup (2 ounces) shredded reduced-fat Cheddar cheese

1. Preheat oven to 350°F. Cut each tortilla into 8 wedges; lightly spray one side of wedges with cooking spray. Place on ungreased baking sheet. Bake for 5 to 9 minutes or until lightly browned and crisp.

2. Cook ground turkey in small nonstick skillet until browned, stirring with spoon to break up meat. Drain fat. Stir in salsa. Cook until hot.

3. Sprinkle meat mixture over tortilla wedges. Sprinkle with green onion. Top with cheese. Return to oven 1 to 2 minutes or until cheese melts.

Makes 4 servings

Serving Suggestion: Cut tortillas into shapes with cookie cutters and bake as directed.

Cook's Note: In a hurry? Substitute baked corn chips for flour tortillas and cooking spray. Proceed as directed.

Cool Candy Cones

Prep Time: 10 minutes

    6 flat-bottom ice cream cones
    1 tub (8 ounces) COOL WHIP® Whipped Topping, thawed
    ⅓ cup multicolored sprinkles
    1 cup chopped candy bars (chocolate-covered wafer bars, peanut
        butter cups, etc.)

SPREAD top rims of ice cream cones with whipped topping. Roll in sprinkles.

STIR candy into remaining topping. Carefully spoon into prepared ice cream cones. Garnish tops with additional chopped candy, if desired. Serve immediately, or refrigerate or freeze until ready to serve.

Makes 6 servings

Berries and Cream: Substitute 1 cup raspberries or chopped strawberries for the chopped candy bars.

Cool Candy Cones

Mexican Flats

2 (6-inch) corn tortillas
½ cup (2 ounces) shredded reduced-fat sharp Cheddar cheese
2 tablespoons nonfat sour cream
¼ cup canned black beans, rinsed and drained
¼ cup salsa
¼ cup sliced ripe olives

1. Place one tortilla on each of two microwavable plates. Sprinkle ¼ cup cheese over each tortilla.

2. Cover each plate with waxed paper and microwave each at HIGH 20 to 30 seconds or until cheese melts.

3. Carefully remove waxed paper. Spread 1 tablespoon sour cream over each tortilla using back of spoon. Top with black beans. Lightly mash beans with fork. Top each flat with salsa and olives. Serve open-face or fold in half like a soft taco.

Makes 2 servings

Finger Lickin' Chicken Salad

½ cup purchased carved roasted skinless chicken breast
½ stalk celery, cut into 1-inch pieces
¼ cup drained mandarin orange segments
¼ cup red seedless grapes
2 tablespoons fat-free sugar-free lemon yogurt
1 tablespoon reduced-fat mayonnaise
¼ teaspoon reduced-sodium soy sauce
⅛ teaspoon pumpkin pie spice or cinnamon

Toss together chicken, celery, orange segments and grapes. Place in covered plastic container. (Or, alternately thread chicken, celery, oranges and grapes on wooden skewers.)

For dipping sauce, stir together yogurt, mayonnaise, soy sauce and pumpkin pie spice.

Pack chicken mixture and dipping sauce in insulated bag with ice pack. To serve, dip chicken mixture into dipping sauce.   *Makes 1 serving*

Refreshers

Prep Time: 5 minutes   *Refrigerating Time:* 4 hours

1 cup boiling water
1 package (4-serving size) JELL-O® Brand
    Gelatin Dessert, any flavor
1 cup cold beverage, such as seltzer, club soda, ginger ale, iced tea
    or lemon-lime carbonated beverage

STIR boiling water into gelatin in medium bowl at least 2 minutes until completely dissolved. Stir in cold beverage.

REFRIGERATE 4 hours or until firm. Cut into cubes and garnish as desired.

Makes 4 servings

Sugar Free Low Calorie Refreshers: Prepare recipe as directed above using any flavor JELL-O® Brand Sugar Free Low Calorie Gelatin Dessert and 1 cup seltzer, club soda, diet ginger ale, diet iced tea or diet lemon-lime carbonated beverage.

JELL-O® Fun Facts: The first JELL-O® flavors—strawberry, raspberry, orange and lemon—are still available today and are among the most popular flavors.

Tortellini Teasers

Zesty Tomato Sauce (recipe follows)
½ (9-ounce) package refrigerated cheese tortellini
1 large red or green bell pepper, cut into 1-inch pieces
2 medium carrots, peeled and sliced ½ inch thick
1 medium zucchini, sliced ½ inch thick
12 medium fresh mushrooms
12 cherry tomatoes

1. Prepare Zesty Tomato Sauce; keep warm.

2. Cook tortellini according to package directions; drain.

3. Alternate 1 tortellini and 2 to 3 vegetable pieces on long frilled wooden picks or wooden skewers. Serve as dippers with tomato sauce.

Makes 6 servings

Zesty Tomato Sauce

1 can (15 ounces) tomato purée
2 tablespoons finely chopped onion
2 tablespoons chopped fresh parsley
1 teaspoon dried oregano leaves
¼ teaspoon dried thyme leaves
¼ teaspoon salt
⅛ teaspoon black pepper

Combine tomato purée, onion, parsley, oregano and thyme in small saucepan. Heat thoroughly, stirring occasionally. Stir in salt and pepper. Garnish with carrot curl, if desired.

Savory Pita Chips

2 whole wheat or white pita bread rounds
   Olive oil-flavored nonstick cooking spray
3 tablespoons grated Parmesan cheese
1 teaspoon dried basil leaves
¼ teaspoon garlic powder

1. Preheat oven to 350°F. Line baking sheet with foil; set aside.

2. Using small scissors, carefully split each pita bread round around edges; separate to form 2 rounds. Cut each round into 6 wedges.

3. Place wedges, rough side down, on prepared baking sheet; coat lightly with cooking spray. Turn wedges over; spray again.

4. Combine Parmesan cheese, basil and garlic powder in small bowl; sprinkle evenly over pita wedges.

5. Bake 12 to 14 minutes or until golden brown. Cool completely.

Makes 4 servings

Cinnamon Crisps: Substitute butter-flavored cooking spray for olive oil-flavored cooking spray, and 1 tablespoon sugar mixed with ¼ teaspoon ground cinnamon for Parmesan cheese, basil and garlic powder.

Chocolate-Caramel S'Mores

**12 chocolate wafer cookies or chocolate graham cracker squares
2 tablespoons fat-free caramel topping
6 large marshmallows**

1. Prepare coals for grilling. Place 6 wafer cookies top-down on a plate. Spread 1 teaspoon caramel topping in center of each wafer to within about ¼-inch of edge.

2. Spear 1 to 2 marshmallows onto long wood-handled skewers.* Hold several inches above coals 3 to 5 minutes until golden and very soft, turning slowly. Push 1 marshmallow off into center of caramel. Top with plain wafer. Repeat with remaining marshmallows and wafers.

Makes 6 servings

*If wood-handled skewers are unavailable, use oven mitt to protect hand from heat.

Cook's Notes: S'mores, a favorite campfire treat, got its name because everyone who tasted them wanted "some more." In the unlikely event of leftover S'mores, they can be reheated in the microwave at HIGH 15 to 30 seconds.

Pudding Chillers

Prep Time: 10 minutes   *Freezing Time:* 5 hours

2 cups cold milk
1 package (4-serving size) JELL-O® Instant Pudding & Pie Filling,
   any flavor
6 (5-ounce) paper cups

POUR milk into medium bowl. Add pudding mix. Beat with wire whisk
2 minutes. Spoon into cups. Insert wooden pop stick into each for a handle.

FREEZE 5 hours or overnight until firm. To remove pop from cup, place
bottom of cup under warm running water for 15 seconds. Press firmly on
bottom of cup to release pop. (Do not twist or pull pop stick.)

Makes 6 pops

Rocky Road: Use JELL-O® Chocolate Flavor Instant Pudding & Pie Filling
and stir in ½ cup miniature marshmallows and ¼ cup each BAKER'S®
Semi-Sweet Real Chocolate Chunks and chopped peanuts.

Toffee Crunch: Use JELL-O® Vanilla Flavor Instant Pudding & Pie Filling
and stir in ½ cup chopped chocolate-covered toffee bars.

Cookies & Cream: Use JELL-O® Vanilla Flavor Instant Pudding & Pie
Filling and stir in ½ cup chopped chocolate sandwich cookies.

Rainbow Spirals

Prep Time: 10 minutes

4 (10-inch) flour tortillas (assorted flavors and colors)
4 tablespoons *French's*® Mustard (any flavor)
½ pound (about 8 slices) thinly sliced deli roast beef, bologna or turkey
8 slices American, provolone or Muenster cheese
Fancy Party Toothpicks

1. Spread each tortilla with *1 tablespoon* mustard. Layer with meat and cheeses dividing evenly.

2. Roll-up jelly-roll style; secure with toothpicks and cut into thirds. Arrange on platter.

Makes 4 to 6 servings

Cheesy Barbecued Bean Dip

½ cup canned vegetarian baked beans
3 tablespoons pasteurized process cheese spread
2 tablespoons regular or hickory smoke barbecue sauce
2 large carrots, cut into diagonal slices
1 medium red or green bell pepper, cut into chunks

1. Place beans in small microwavable bowl; mash slightly with fork. Stir in process cheese spread and barbecue sauce. Cover with vented plastic wrap.

2. Microwave at HIGH 1 minute; stir. Microwave 30 seconds or until hot. Garnish with green onion and bell pepper cutouts, if desired. Serve with carrot and bell pepper dippers.

Makes 4 servings

JELL-O® Glazed Popcorn

Prep Time: 10 minutes   *Cook Time:* 15 minutes

 8 cups popped popcorn
 1 cup salted peanuts or cashews
 ¼ cup butter or margarine
 3 tablespoons light corn syrup
 ½ cup packed light brown sugar or granulated sugar
 1 package (4-serving size) JELL-O® Brand Gelatin, any flavor

HEAT oven to 300°F. Line a 15×10×1-inch pan with foil or waxed paper. Place popcorn and nuts in large bowl.

HEAT butter and syrup in small saucepan over low heat. Stir in sugar and gelatin; bring to a boil on medium heat. Reduce heat to low and gently simmer for 5 minutes. Immediately pour syrup over popcorn, tossing to coat well.

SPREAD popcorn in prepared pan, using two forks to spread evenly. Bake 10 minutes. Cool. Remove from pan and break into small pieces.

Makes about 9 cups

Delicious Drinks

Citrus Cooler

Prep Time: 5 minutes

1 envelope KOOL-AID® Sugar Free Lemonade Flavor Low
    Calorie Soft Drink Mix
2 cups cold water
2 cups cold orange juice
1 bottle (1 liter) cold diet lemon-lime carbonated beverage
    Ice cubes

PLACE drink mix in large plastic or glass pitcher. Add water and juice; stir to dissolve. Refrigerate until ready to serve.

JUST before serving, stir in carbonated beverage. Serve over ice.

Makes 8 (1-cup) servings

Chocolaty-Rich Hot Cocoa

Prep Time: 10 minutes

1 package (4-serving size) JELL-O® Chocolate Flavor Cook & Serve
    Pudding & Pie Filling (not Instant)
1½ quarts milk
½ cup BAKER'S® Semi-Sweet Chocolate Chunks
½ teaspoon vanilla
    Thawed COOL WHIP® Whipped Topping *or* JET-PUFFED®
    Miniature Marshmallows (optional)

STIR pudding mix and milk in medium saucepan with wire whisk until blended. Stirring constantly, cook over medium heat until mixture comes to full boil. Remove from heat. Add chocolate chunks and vanilla. Stir with wire whisk until well blended.

POUR into mugs and garnish with a dollop of whipped topping or several marshmallows. Serve immediately. *Makes 6 servings*

How To: Mixture will thicken as it stands. To thin, just add more milk and reheat.

Citrus Punch

    Frozen Fruit Ice (recipe follows)
2 cups orange juice
2 cups grapefruit juice
¾ cup lime juice
½ cup light corn syrup
1 bottle (750 mL) ginger ale, white grape juice, Asti Spumante or
    sparkling wine
    Fresh mint sprigs for garnish
4 oranges, sectioned
1 to 2 limes, cut into ⅛-inch slices
1 lemon, cut into ⅛-inch slices
1 pint strawberries, stemmed and halved
1 cup raspberries

Prepare Frozen Fruit Ice.

Combine juices and corn syrup in 2-quart pitcher. Stir until corn syrup dissolves. (Stir in additional corn syrup to taste.) Refrigerate 2 hours or until cold. Stir in ginger ale just before serving.

Divide Frozen Fruit Ice between 8 (12-ounce) glasses or 10 wide-rimmed wine glasses. Fill glasses with punch. Garnish, if desired. Serve immediately.

Makes 8 to 10 servings (about 5 cups)

Frozen Fruit Ice: Spread oranges, limes, lemon, strawberries and raspberries on baking sheet. Freeze 4 hours or until firm.

Fruit Smoothies

1 cup orange juice
1 cup fat-free plain yogurt
1 frozen banana*
1 cup frozen strawberries or raspberries
1¾ teaspoons EQUAL® FOR RECIPES *or* 6 packets EQUAL®
  sweetener *or* ¼ cup EQUAL® SPOONFUL™

*Peel and cut banana into large chunks. Place in plastic freezer bag, seal and freeze at least 5 to 6 hours or overnight.

• Place all ingredients in blender or food processor. Blend until smooth.

Makes 2 servings

Creepy Crawler Punch

1 Creepy Crawler Ice Ring (recipe follows)
2 cups corn syrup
¼ cup water
6 cinnamon sticks
2 tablespoons whole cloves
½ teaspoon ground allspice
2 quarts cranberry juice cocktail
1 quart orange juice
1½ quarts pineapple juice
½ cup lemon juice
2 quarts ginger ale

1. The night or day before serving, prepare Creepy Crawler Ice Ring.

2. Stir together corn syrup and water in medium saucepan over medium-high heat. Add cinnamon sticks, cloves and allspice, and stir gently. Bring to a boil and immediately reduce heat to a simmer; simmer 10 minutes.

3. Refrigerate, covered, until chilled. Remove cinnamon sticks and discard. Strain out cloves and discard.

4. In punch bowl, combine syrup mixture with juices and ginger ale. Unmold Creepy Crawler Ice Ring and add to punch bowl.

Makes 36 servings

Creepy Crawler Ice Ring

1 cup gummy worms or other creepy crawler candy
1 quart lemon-lime thirst quencher beverage

• Arrange gummy worms in bottom of 5-cup ring mold; fill mold with thirst quencher beverage. Freeze until solid, 8 hours or overnight.

"Moo-vin" Milk Shakes

Chocolate Shake

1 pint low-fat sugar-free chocolate ice cream
½ cup fat-free (skim) milk
1 tablespoon chocolate syrup
¼ teaspoon vanilla
⅛ teaspoon decorator sprinkles (optional)

Chocolate Cherry Shake

1 pint low-fat sugar-free chocolate ice cream
¾ drained canned pitted tart red cherries
¼ cup fat-free (skim) milk
¼ teaspoon vanilla
⅛ teaspoon decorator sprinkles (optional)

Chocolate-Peanut Butter Shake

1 pint low-fat sugar-free chocolate ice cream
½ cup fat-free (skim) milk
¼ cup creamy peanut butter
¼ teaspoon vanilla
⅛ teaspoon decorator sprinkles (optional)

Vanilla Shake

1 pint low-fat sugar-free vanilla ice cream
½ cup fat-free (skim) milk
½ teaspoon vanilla
⅛ teaspoon decorator sprinkles (optional)

Strawberry Shake

1 pint low-fat sugar-free vanilla ice cream
1 cup frozen unsweetened strawberries, thawed
¼ cup fat-free (skim) milk
¼ teaspoon vanilla

For any flavor shake, combine all ingredients except decorator sprinkles in blender container. Cover and blend until smooth. Pour into 2 small glasses. Add decorator sprinkles, if desired. Serve immediately.   *Makes 2 servings*

Magic Potion

Creepy Crawler Ice Ring (recipe page 54)
1 cup boiling water
2 packages (4-serving size each) lime-flavored gelatin
3 cups cold water
1½ quarts carbonated lemon-lime beverage, chilled
½ cup superfine sugar
Gummy worms (optional)

• One day ahead, prepare Creepy Crawler Ice Ring.

• Pour boiling water over gelatin in heatproof punch bowl; stir until gelatin dissolves. Stir in cold water. Add lemon-lime beverage and sugar; stir well (mixture will foam for several minutes).

• Unmold ice ring by dipping bottom of mold briefly into hot water. Float ice ring in punch. Serve cups of punch garnished with gummy worms, if desired.

Makes about 10 servings

Haunted Hint: Change this Magic Potion from creepy to cute with just a few simple substitutions. For the punch, use orange-flavored gelatin instead of lime. For the ice ring, use candy corn and candy pumpkins instead of gummy worms.

Sparkling Apple Punch

2 bottles (750 ml each) sparkling apple cider, chilled
1½ quarts papaya or apricot nectar, chilled
　Ice
1 or 2 papayas, peeled and chopped
　Orange slices, quartered

Combine apple cider, papaya nectar and ice in punch bowl. Add papaya and orange slices.

Makes about 4 quarts

Mocha Colada

3 ounces MR & MRS T® Piña Colada Mix
1 ounce COCO CASA® Cream of Coconut
2 ounces cold espresso (or other strong coffee)
1 cup ice
½ tablespoon chocolate syrup
　Chocolate covered espresso bean, for garnish

Blend first 4 ingredients in blender until slushy. Pour into tall glass and garnish with chocolate syrup and espresso bean.

Makes 1 serving

Bottom to top: Sparkling Apple Punch, Citrus Punch (page 51)

Sunrise Punch

Prep Time: 5 minutes plus refrigerating

1 tub **CRYSTAL LIGHT TROPICAL PASSIONS®** Strawberry Kiwi
    Flavor Low Calorie Soft Drink Mix
2 cups cold water
2 cups chilled unsweetened pineapple juice
1 bottle (1 liter) chilled seltzer
  Ice cubes

PLACE drink mix in large plastic or glass pitcher. Add water and juice; stir to dissolve. Refrigerate.

JUST before serving, pour into large punch bowl. Stir in seltzer. Serve over ice.
Makes 2 quarts or 8 (1-cup) servings

Sunrise Punch

Super Cherry Cola Floats

Prep Time: 15 minutes plus refrigerating

1 cup boiling water
1 package (4-serving size) JELL-O® Brand Cherry Flavor Gelatin
1¼ cups cold cola
1 pint vanilla ice cream (2 cups)

STIR boiling water into gelatin in medium bowl 2 minutes until completely dissolved. Stir in cola. Refrigerate 20 to 30 minutes or until slightly thickened (consistency of unbeaten egg whites). Reserve ½ cup gelatin.

PLACE ½ cup ice cream into each of 4 tall ice cream soda glasses. Top with thickened gelatin mixture.

BEAT reserved ½ cup gelatin mixture with electric mixer on medium speed until light and fluffy. Spoon into each glass.

REFRIGERATE 2 hours or until firm.   *Makes 4 servings*

Special Extra: Garnish each float with a maraschino cherry and sprinkles.

Super Cherry Cola Float

Country Time® Lemon Berry Cooler

Prep Time: 5 minutes

1 cup prepared **COUNTRY TIME®** Lemonade Flavor Sugar Free
    Low Calorie Drink Mix
½ cup cold 2% reduced-fat milk
½ cup strawberry or raspberry sorbet or sherbet
½ cup ice cubes or crushed ice

PLACE all ingredients in blender container; cover. Blend on high speed
until smooth. Serve immediately.   *Makes 2 (1-cup) servings*

Country Time® Lemon Creamy Frosty

Prep Time: 5 minutes

1 cup prepared **COUNTRY TIME®** Lemonade Flavor Sugar Free
    Low Calorie Drink Mix
1 cup no-sugar-added vanilla ice cream
½ cup ice cubes or crushed ice

PLACE all ingredients in blender container; cover. Blend on high speed
about 30 seconds or until thickened and smooth. Serve immediately.
                                                    Makes 2 (1-cup) servings

Bottom to Top: Country Time® Lemon Berry Cooler,
Country Time® Lemon Creamy Frosty

Snowbird Mocktails

Prep time: 10 minutes

3 cups pineapple juice
1 can (14 ounces) sweetened condensed milk
1 can (6 ounces) frozen orange juice concentrate, thawed
½ teaspoon coconut extract
1 bottle (32 ounces) ginger ale, chilled

1. Combine pineapple juice, sweetened condensed milk, orange juice concentrate and coconut extract in large pitcher; stir well. Refrigerate, covered, up to 1 week.

2. To serve, pour ½ cup pineapple juice mixture into individual glasses (over crushed ice, if desired). Top off each glass with about ⅓ cup ginger ale.

Makes 10 servings

Tip: Store unopened cans of sweetened condensed milk at room temperature up to 6 months. Once opened, store in airtight container in refrigerator for up to 5 days.

Fizzy Cran-Grape Lemonade Punch

Prep Time: 10 minutes

1 envelope KOOL-AID® Sugar Free Lemonade Flavor Low Calorie
   Soft Drink Mix
1 bottle (48 ounces) chilled reduced-calorie cranberry-grape juice
   cocktail
1 bottle (1 liter) chilled seltzer
1 navel orange, sliced, cut into quarters
   Ice cubes or crushed ice

PLACE drink mix in large plastic or glass pitcher. Add cranberry-grape juice cocktail; stir to dissolve. Refrigerate.

POUR into large punch bowl just before serving. Stir in seltzer and oranges. Serve over ice.   *Makes 2½ quarts or 10 (1-cup) servings*

Key Lime Smoothie

Prep Time: 10 minutes

½ cup boiling water
1 package (4-serving size) JELL-O® Brand Lime Flavor Gelatin
1 cup ice cubes
Cold water
1½ cups thawed COOL WHIP® Whipped Topping

STIR boiling water into gelatin in medium bowl at least 2 minutes until completely dissolved. Mix ice and enough cold water to make 1½ cups.

POUR gelatin, ice water and whipped topping into blender container; cover. Blend on medium speed until smooth. Serve immediately.

Makes 4 servings

Special Extras: Garnish each smoothie with a fresh whole strawberry and a large dollop of thawed COOL WHIP® Whipped Topping.

Great Substitute: Try any flavor JELL-O® Brand Gelatin for a delicious treat!

Monkey Shake (page 76) and Key Lime Smoothie

Merry Mango Fizz

1 bottle (64 ounces) MAUNA LA'I® ¡Mango Mango!® Juice Drink
1 bottle (32 ounces) cranberry juice cocktail
1 bottle (32 ounces) ginger ale
2 cups vanilla ice cream
   Fresh or frozen strawberries, as needed

Combine Mauna La'i ¡Mango Mango! Juice Drink and cranberry juice cocktail in large punch bowl. Fifteen minutes before serving, add ginger ale and ice cream. Do not stir. Garnish with strawberries.   *Makes 24 servings*

Toasted Coco Colada

3 ounces MR & MRS T® Piña Colada Mix
1½ ounces coconut milk
½ ounce caramel syrup
½ ounce coconut syrup
1 cup ice
1 lime wedge
   Toasted coconut flakes, ground (as needed)

Blend first 5 ingredients in blender until slushy. Coat rim of daiquiri glass with lime wedge; dip glass into ground toasted coconut flakes. Pour into daiquiri glass.   *Makes 1 drink*

Merry Mango Fizz, Mocha Colada (page 60) and Toasted Coco Colada

Goblin Shake

1 tub (8 ounces) COOL WHIP® Whipped Topping, thawed
1 can (6 ounces) frozen orange juice concentrate, thawed
1 juice can water (¾ cup)
1½ cups crushed ice
    Few drops red and yellow food coloring
    Candy corn and pumpkins
    Additional thawed COOL WHIP® Whipped Topping

PLACE 1 tub whipped topping, juice concentrate, water, ice and food coloring in blender container; cover. Blend on high speed 1 minute or until smooth. Pour into glasses. Garnish with additional whipped topping and candies. Serve immediately.

Makes 4 servings

Berry-Banana Breakfast Smoothie

1 carton (8 ounces) berry-flavored yogurt
1 ripe banana, cut into chunks
½ cup milk

Place all ingredients in blender. Cover; blend until smooth.

Makes about 2 cups

Magical Meals

Zippity Hot Doggity Tacos

Prep Time: 5 minutes   *Cook Time:* 8 minutes

1 small onion, finely chopped
1 tablespoon *Frank's® RedHot®* Cayenne Pepper Sauce or
    French's® Worcestershire Sauce
4 frankfurters, chopped
1 can (10½ ounces) red kidney or black beans, drained
1 can (8 ounces) tomato sauce
1 teaspoon chili powder
8 taco shells, heated
1 cup *French's®* French Fried Onions
    Garnish: chopped tomatoes, shredded lettuce, sliced olives,
        sour cream, shredded cheese

1. Heat *1 tablespoon oil* in 12-inch nonstick skillet over medium-high heat. Cook onion, 3 minutes or until crisp-tender. Stir in remaining ingredients. Bring to boiling. Reduce heat to medium-low and cook 5 minutes, stirring occasionally.

2. To serve, spoon chili into taco shells. Garnish as desired and sprinkle with **French Fried Onions**. Splash on **Frank's RedHot** Sauce for extra zip!
Makes 4 servings

Little Piggy Pies

Prep Time: 10 minutes   *Bake Time:* 11 minutes

2 cups frozen mixed soup vegetables (carrots, potatoes, peas,
   celery, green beans, corn, onions and lima beans)
1 (10¾-ounce) can reduced-fat condensed cream of chicken soup,
   undiluted
8 ounces chopped cooked chicken
⅓ cup plain low-fat yogurt
⅓ cup water
½ teaspoon dried thyme leaves
¼ teaspoon poultry seasoning or ground sage
⅛ teaspoon garlic powder
1 (7½-ounce) tube (10) refrigerated buttermilk biscuits

Preheat oven to 400°F. Remove 10 green peas from frozen mixed vegetables. Stir together remaining frozen vegetables, soup, chicken, yogurt, water, thyme, poultry seasoning and garlic powder in medium saucepan. Bring to a boil, stirring frequently. Cover; keep warm.

Press five of the biscuits into 3-inch circles. Cut each remaining biscuit into eight wedges. Place two wedges on top of each circle; fold points down to form ears. Roll one wedge into small ball; place in center of each circle to form pig's snout. Use tip of spoon handle to make indents in snout for nostrils. Place 2 reserved green peas on each circle for eyes.

Spoon hot chicken mixture into 5 (10-ounce) custard cups. Place one biscuit "pig" on top of each. Bake 9 to 11 minutes or until biscuits are golden.   *Makes 5 servings*

Little Piggy Pie

Sloppy Joe's Bun Buggy

4 hot dog buns (not split)
16 thin slices cucumber or zucchini
4 ripe olives or pimiento-stuffed olives
24 thin strips julienned carrots, 1 inch long
   Nonstick cooking spray
1 (10-ounce) package extra-lean ground turkey
1¼ cups bottled reduced-fat spaghetti sauce
½ cup chopped broccoli stems
2 teaspoons prepared mustard
½ teaspoon Worcestershire sauce
   Dash salt
   Dash black pepper
4 small pretzel twists

Hollow out hot dog buns. Use wooden pick to make four holes in sides of each bun to attach "wheels." Use wooden pick to make one hole in center of each cucumber slice; push carrot strip through hole. Press into holes in buns, making "wheels" on buns.

Cut each olive in half horizontally. Use wooden pick to make two holes in one end of each bun to attach "headlights." Use carrot strips to attach olives to buns, making "headlights."

Spray large nonstick skillet with cooking spray. Cook turkey in skillet over medium heat until no longer pink. Stir in spaghetti sauce, broccoli stems, mustard, Worcestershire, salt and black pepper; heat through. Spoon mixture into hollowed-out buns. Press pretzel twist into ground turkey mixture, making "windshield" on each buggy.   *Makes 4 servings*

Silly Spaghetti Casserole

    8 ounces dried spaghetti
¼ cup egg substitute
¼ cup finely shredded Parmesan cheese
½ of 10-ounce package frozen cut spinach, thawed
¾ pound turkey or lean ground beef
⅓ cup chopped onion
    2 bottles spaghetti sauce
¾ cup shredded part-skim mozzarella cheese (3 ounces)
    1 green or yellow bell pepper

Preheat oven to 350°F. Spray an 8-inch square baking dish with nonstick cooking spray. Cook spaghetti according to package directions, omitting salt and oil; drain. Toss with egg substitute and Parmesan cheese. Place in bottom of prepared baking dish.

Drain spinach in colander, pressing out excess liquid. Spray large nonstick skillet with cooking spray. Cook turkey and onion in skillet over medium-high heat until meat is lightly browned, stirring to break up meat. Drain off any fat. Stir in spinach. Stir in spaghetti sauce. Spoon on top of spaghetti mixture in dish.

Sprinkle with mozzarella cheese. Use small cookie cutter to cut decorative shapes from bell pepper. Place on top of cheese in baking dish. Cover with foil. Bake 40 to 45 minutes or until bubbling. Let stand 10 minutes. Cut into squares.

Makes 6 servings

Cheesy Tuna Mac

8 ounces uncooked elbow macaroni
2 tablespoons margarine or butter
2 tablespoons all-purpose flour
1 teaspoon paprika
¼ teaspoon salt
1 cup canned reduced-sodium chicken broth
6 ounces reduced-fat reduced-sodium cheese spread, cut into cubes
1 can (6 ounces) tuna packed in water, drained and flaked

1. Cook macaroni according to package directions, omitting salt. Drain; set aside.

2. Melt margarine in medium saucepan over medium heat. Add flour, paprika and salt; cook and stir 1 minute. Add broth; bring to a simmer for 2 minutes or until sauce thickens.

3. Add cheese spread; cook and stir until cheese melts. Combine tuna and pasta in medium bowl; pour sauce mixture over tuna mixture; toss to coat. Garnish with additional paprika, if desired. *Makes 4 servings*

Cheesy Tuna Mac

Countdown Casserole

1 jar (8 ounces) pasteurized process cheese spread
¾ cup milk
2 cups (12 ounces) cubed cooked roast beef
1 bag (16 ounces) frozen vegetable combination (broccoli, corn, red pepper), thawed and drained
4 cups frozen hash brown potatoes, thawed
1⅓ cups *French's*® French Fried Onions, divided
½ teaspoon seasoned salt
¼ teaspoon freshly ground black pepper
½ cup (2 ounces) shredded Cheddar cheese

Preheat oven to 375°F. Spoon cheese spread into 12×8-inch baking dish; place in oven just until cheese melts, about 5 minutes. Using fork, stir milk into melted cheese until well blended. Stir in beef, vegetables, potatoes, ⅔ cup **French Fried Onions** and the seasonings. Bake, covered, at 375°F 30 minutes or until heated through. Top with Cheddar cheese; sprinkle remaining ⅔ *cup* **French Fried Onions** down center. Bake, uncovered, 3 minutes or until **French Fried Onions** are golden brown.

Makes 4 to 6 servings

Microwave Directions: In 12×8-inch microwave-safe dish, combine cheese spread and milk. Cook, covered, on HIGH 3 minutes; stir. Add ingredients as directed. Cook, covered, 14 minutes or until heated through, stirring beef mixture halfway through cooking time. Top with Cheddar cheese and remaining ⅔ cup onions as directed. Cook, uncovered, 1 minute or until cheese melts. Let stand 5 minutes.

Chili Dogs

½ pound lean ground beef
1 cup chopped onions
1 can (6 ounces) HUNT'S® Tomato Paste No Salt Added
1 cup water
2 tablespoons GEBHARDT® Chili Powder
1 tablespoon prepared yellow mustard
½ teaspoon garlic powder
½ teaspoon ground cumin
¼ teaspoon sugar
⅛ teaspoon crushed red pepper
1 pound BUTTERBALL® Turkey Franks
10 hot dog buns

In skillet, brown beef and onions. Stir in tomato paste, water, chili powder, mustard, garlic powder, cumin, sugar and crushed red pepper; heat through. Meanwhile, heat or grill hot dogs. To serve, place hot dogs in buns; spoon chili down center of each.

Makes 10 chili dogs

Octo-Dogs and Shells

4 hot dogs
1½ cups uncooked small shell pasta
1½ cups frozen mixed vegetables
1 cup prepared Alfredo sauce
   Prepared yellow mustard in squeeze bottle
   Cheese-flavored fish-shaped crackers

Lay 1 hot dog on side with end facing you. Starting 1 inch from one end of hot dog, slice hot dog vertically in half. Roll hot dog ¼ turn and slice in half vertically again, making 4 segments connected at the top. Slice each segment in half vertically, creating a total of 8 "legs." Repeat with remaining hot dogs.

Place hot dogs in medium saucepan; cover with water. Bring to a boil over medium-high heat. Remove from heat; set aside.

Prepare pasta according to package directions, stirring in vegetables during last 3 minutes of cooking time. Drain; return to pan. Stir in Alfredo sauce. Heat over low heat until heated through. Divide pasta mixture between four plates.

Drain octo-dogs. Arrange one octo-dog on top of pasta mixture on each plate. Draw faces on "heads" of octo-dogs with mustard. Sprinkle crackers over pasta mixture.

Makes 4 servings

Family Favorite Hamburger Casserole

1 tablespoon CRISCO® Oil* plus additional for oiling
1 cup chopped onion
1 pound ground beef round
1 package (9 ounces) frozen cut green beans
3 cups frozen southern style hash brown potatoes
1 can (10¾ ounces) zesty tomato soup
½ cup water
1 teaspoon dried basil leaves
¾ teaspoon salt
¼ teaspoon pepper
¼ cup plain dry bread crumbs

Use your favorite Crisco Oil product.

1. Heat oven to 350°F. Oil 11¾×7½×2-inch baking dish lightly. Place cooling rack on countertop.

2. Heat oil in large skillet on medium-high heat. Add onion. Cook and stir until tender. Add meat. Cook until browned, stirring occasionally. Add beans. Cook and stir 5 minutes or until thawed. Add potatoes.

3. Combine tomato soup and water in small bowl. Stir until well blended. Stir into skillet. Stir in basil, salt and pepper. Spoon into baking dish. Sprinkle with bread crumbs.

4. Bake at 350°F for 30 minutes or until potatoes are tender. *Do not overbake.* Let stand 5 minutes before serving.

Makes 4 servings

Devilish Delights

1 package (16 ounces) hot roll mix plus ingredients to prepare mix
1 pound boneless skinless chicken breasts, cut into ¾-inch pieces
2 tablespoons vegetable oil, divided
¾ cup chopped onion
1 clove garlic, minced
1¼ cups sliced zucchini
1 can (8 ounces) peeled diced tomatoes, drained
1 can (4 ounces) sliced mushrooms, drained
1 teaspoon dried basil leaves
½ teaspoon dried oregano leaves
Salt and black pepper
1 cup (4 ounces) shredded mozzarella cheese
1 egg yolk
1 teaspoon water
Red food color

1. Prepare hot roll mix according to package directions. Knead dough on lightly floured surface until smooth, about 5 minutes. Cover loosely; let stand about 15 minutes.

2. Cook chicken in 1 tablespoon oil in large skillet over medium-high heat 5 to 6 minutes or until no longer pink in center; remove from skillet and set aside. Cook and stir onion and garlic in remaining 1 tablespoon oil in skillet until tender.

3. Stir in zucchini, tomatoes, mushrooms, basil and oregano; bring to a boil. Reduce heat; simmer 5 to 10 minutes or until excess liquid has evaporated. Stir in reserved chicken; cook 1 minute. Remove from heat; season to taste with salt and pepper. Stir in cheese.

4. Preheat oven to 400°F. Grease baking sheets.

5. Roll dough on floured surface to ¼-inch thickness. Cut into equal number of 4-inch circles. Combine scraps and reroll dough if necessary. Place half of circles on prepared baking sheets. Spoon about ¼ cup chicken mixture on half the circles; top with remaining circles and seal edges with fork. Cut vents to resemble devil and use dough scraps to make horns, eyes, nose and beard.

6. Combine egg yolk and water; brush dough. Add red food color to remaining egg yolk mixture. Brush horns and beard with colored egg mixture.

7. Bake 20 to 25 minutes or until golden. Refrigerate leftovers. *Makes 10 to 12 servings*

Lit'l Smokies 'n' Macaroni 'n' Cheese

1 package (7¼ ounces) macaroni and cheese mix, prepared
    according to package directions
1 pound HILLSHIRE FARM® Lit'l Smokies
1 can (10¾ ounces) condensed cream of celery or mushroom soup,
    undiluted
⅓ cup milk
1 tablespoon minced parsley (optional)
1 cup (4 ounces) shredded Cheddar cheese

Preheat oven to 350°F.

Combine prepared macaroni and cheese, Lit'l Smokies, soup, milk and
parsley, if desired, in medium bowl. Pour into small greased casserole.
Sprinkle Cheddar cheese over top. Bake, uncovered, 20 minutes or until
heated through. *Makes 8 servings*

Maple Francheezies

    Mustard Spread (recipe follows)
¼ **cup maple syrup**
2 **teaspoons garlic powder**
1 **teaspoon black pepper**
½ **teaspoon ground nutmeg**
4 **slices bacon**
4 **jumbo hot dogs**
4 **hot dog buns, split**
½ **cup (2 ounces) shredded Cheddar cheese**

Prepare Mustard Spread; set aside.

Prepare grill for direct cooking.

Combine maple syrup, garlic powder, pepper and nutmeg in small bowl. Brush syrup mixture onto bacon slices. Wrap 1 slice bacon around each hot dog.

Brush hot dogs with remaining syrup mixture. Place hot dogs on grid. Grill, covered, over medium-high heat 8 minutes or until bacon is crisp and hot dogs are heated through, turning halfway through grilling time. Place hot dogs in buns, top with Mustard Spread and cheese. *Makes 4 servings*

Mustard Spread

½ **cup prepared yellow mustard**
1 **tablespoon finely chopped onion**
1 **tablespoon diced tomato**
1 **tablespoon chopped fresh parsley**
1 **teaspoon garlic powder**
½ **teaspoon black pepper**

Combine all ingredients in small bowl; mix well. *Makes about ¾ cup*

Maple Francheezie

Cheesy Mustard Dip

Prep Time: 15 minutes

1 container (8 ounces) whipped cream cheese
¼ cup milk
3 tablespoons *French's*® Hearty Deli Brown or Honey Mustard
2 tablespoons mayonnaise
2 tablespoons minced green onions

1. Combine ingredients for dip in medium bowl; mix until well blended.

Makes 8 servings (about 1¼ cups dip)

Zesty Fun Pretzel Dip

Prep Time: 5 minutes

½ cup *French's*® Zesty Deli Mustard
½ cup honey

1. Combine mustard and honey.
2. Use for dipping pretzels, chips or cheese cubes.

Makes 1 cup

Clockwise from left: Cheesy Mustard Dip,
Zesty Fun Pretzel Dip, French's® Honey Mustard

Cheeseburger Macaroni

Prep Time: 8 minutes   *Cook Time:* 15 minutes

1 cup mostaccioli or elbow macaroni, uncooked
1 pound ground beef
1 medium onion, chopped
1 can (14½ ounces) DEL MONTE® Diced Tomatoes with Basil,
    Garlic & Oregano
¼ cup DEL MONTE Tomato Ketchup
1 cup (4 ounces) shredded Cheddar cheese

1. Cook pasta according to package directions; drain.

2. Brown meat with onion in large skillet; drain. Season with salt and pepper, if desired. Stir in undrained tomatoes, ketchup and pasta; heat through.

3. Top with cheese. Garnish, if desired.   *Makes 4 servings*

Mom's Tuna Casserole

2 cans (12 ounces each) tuna, drained and flaked
3 cups diced celery
3 cups crushed potato chips, divided
6 hard-cooked eggs, chopped
1 can (10¾ ounces) condensed cream of mushroom soup,
    undiluted
1 can (10¾ ounces) condensed cream of celery soup, undiluted
1 cup mayonnaise
1 teaspoon dried tarragon leaves
1 teaspoon black pepper

Slow Cooker Directions
Combine all ingredients, except ½ cup potato chips, in slow cooker; stir well. Top mixture with remaining ½ cup potato chips. Cover and cook on Low 5 to 8 hours.

Makes 8 servings

Western Wagon Wheels

Prep Time: 25 minutes   *Cook Time:* 5 minutes

1 pound lean ground beef or ground turkey
2 cups wagon wheel pasta, uncooked
1 can (14½ ounces) stewed tomatoes
1½ cups water
1 box (10 ounces) BIRDS EYE® frozen Sweet Corn
½ cup barbecue sauce
Salt and pepper to taste

• In large skillet, cook beef over medium heat 5 minutes or until well browned.

• Stir in pasta, tomatoes, water, corn and barbecue sauce; bring to boil.

• Reduce heat to low; cover and simmer 15 to 20 minutes or until pasta is tender, stirring occasionally. Season with salt and pepper.

Makes 4 servings

Serving Suggestion: Serve with corn bread or corn muffins.

Skillet Spaghetti and Sausage

Prep Time: 5 minutes   *Cook Time:* 30 minutes

¼ pound mild or hot Italian sausage links, sliced
½ pound ground beef
¼ teaspoon dried oregano, crushed
4 ounces spaghetti, broken in half
1 can (14½ ounces) DEL MONTE® Diced Tomatoes with Basil,
    Garlic & Oregano
1 can (8 ounces) DEL MONTE Tomato Sauce
1½ cups sliced fresh mushrooms
2 stalks celery, sliced

1. Brown sausage in large skillet over medium-high heat. Add beef and oregano; season to taste with salt and pepper, if desired.

2. Cook, stirring occasionally, until beef is browned; drain.

3. Add pasta, 1 cup water, undrained tomatoes, tomato sauce, mushrooms and celery. Bring to boil, stirring occasionally.

4. Reduce heat; cover and simmer 12 to 14 minutes or until spaghetti is tender. Garnish with grated Parmesan cheese and chopped parsley, if desired. Serve immediately.   *Makes 4 to 6 servings*

Hot Diggity Dogs

Prep Time: 5 minutes   *Cook Time:* 20 minutes

2 tablespoons butter or margarine
2 large (1 pound) sweet onions, thinly sliced
½ cup *French's*® Classic Yellow® Mustard
½ cup ketchup
10 frankfurters
10 frankfurter buns

Melt butter in medium skillet over medium heat. Add onion; cook
10 minutes or until very tender, stirring often. Stir in mustard and ketchup.
Cook over low heat 2 minutes, stirring often.

Place frankfurters and buns on grid. Grill over medium coals 5 minutes or
until frankfurters are browned and buns are toasted, turning once. To serve,
spoon onion mixture into buns; top each with 1 frankfurter.

Makes 10 servings (about 2½ cups onion topping)

Tip: Onion topping is also great on hamburgers or smoked sausage heros.

Turkey and Macaroni

    1 teaspoon vegetable oil
1½ pounds ground turkey
    2 cans (10¾ ounces each) condensed tomato soup, undiluted
    2 cups uncooked macaroni, cooked and drained
    1 can (16 ounces) corn, drained
    ½ cup chopped onion
    1 can (4 ounces) sliced mushrooms, drained
    2 tablespoons ketchup
    1 tablespoon mustard
    Salt and black pepper to taste

Slow Cooker Directions

Heat oil in medium skillet; cook turkey until browned. Transfer mixture to slow cooker. Add remaining ingredients to slow cooker. Stir to blend. Cover and cook on LOW 7 to 9 hours or on HIGH 3 to 4 hours.

Makes 4 to 6 servings

Tacos Olé

Prep Time: 5 minutes   *Cook Time:* 10 minutes

1 pound ground beef or turkey
1 cup salsa
¼ cup *Frank's*® *RedHot*® Cayenne Pepper Sauce
2 teaspoons chili powder
8 taco shells, heated
   Garnish: chopped tomatoes, shredded lettuce, sliced olives, sour cream, shredded cheese

1. Cook beef in skillet over medium-high heat 5 minutes or until browned, stirring to separate meat; drain. Stir in salsa, **Frank's RedHot** Sauce and chili powder. Heat to boiling. Reduce heat to medium-low. Cook 5 minutes, stirring often.

2. To serve, spoon meat mixture into taco shells. Splash on more **Frank's RedHot** Sauce to taste. Garnish as desired.   *Makes 4 servings*

Chicken Enchilada Skillet Casserole

Prep Time: 5 minutes   *Cook Time:* 10 minutes

1 bag (16 ounces) BIRDS EYE® frozen Farm Fresh Mixtures
   Broccoli, Corn & Red Peppers
1 package (1¼ ounces) taco seasoning mix
1 can (16 ounces) diced tomatoes, undrained
3 cups shredded cooked chicken
1 cup shredded Monterey Jack cheese
8 ounces tortilla chips

• In large skillet, combine vegetables, seasoning mix, tomatoes and chicken; bring to boil over medium-high heat.

• Cover; cook 4 minutes or until vegetables are cooked and mixture is heated through.

• Sprinkle with cheese; cover and cook 2 minutes more or until cheese is melted.

• Serve with chips.   *Makes 4 servings*

Birds Eye Idea: Here's a quick lunch item for kids. Cut up 4 cooked hot dogs; stir into 1 bag of prepared Birds Eye® Pasta Secrets White Cheddar.

Surfin' Salmon

⅓ cup egg substitute
⅓ cup cornflake crumbs
2 tablespoons fat-free (skim) milk
¾ teaspoon dried dill weed
⅛ teaspoon black pepper
    Dash hot pepper sauce
1 (14½-ounce) can salmon, drained and skin and bones removed
    Nonstick cooking spray
1 teaspoon olive oil
5 small pieces pimiento
6 tablespoons purchased tartar sauce

Stir together egg substitute, cornflake crumbs, milk, dill weed, black pepper and hot pepper sauce in large mixing bowl. Add salmon; mix well.

Spray large nonstick skillet with cooking spray. Shape salmon mixture into 5 large egg-shaped balls. Flatten each into ¾-inch-thick oval. Pinch one end of each oval into tail shape for fish.

Cook in skillet over medium-high heat 2 to 3 minutes or until lightly browned; turn. Add oil to skillet. Continue cooking 2 to 3 minutes or until firm and lightly browned. Place small drop tartar sauce and pimiento on each for "eye." Serve with tartar sauce.   *Makes 5 servings*

Barbecue Flying Saucers with Vegetable Martians

    1 (10-ounce) pork tenderloin
    ½ teaspoon black pepper*
    ¼ cup barbecue sauce
    ½ teaspoon prepared mustard
    1 (7½-ounce) tube (10) refrigerated buttermilk biscuits
    1 egg yolk (optional)
    1 teaspoon water (optional)
    3 to 4 drops food coloring (optional)
    Vegetable Martians (recipe follows)

Substitute 10 ounces lean deli roasted pork for pork tenderloin and pepper, if desired.

Preheat oven to 425°F. Rub pepper on outside of pork tenderloin. Place pork in shallow roasting pan. Roast 15 to 25 minutes or until meat thermometer inserted into thickest part of meat registers 160° F. Let stand 5 minutes. Using 2 forks, shred pork.

Reduce oven temperature to 400°F. Stir together barbecue sauce and mustard. Toss with shredded pork.

Roll each biscuit on lightly floured surface into 4-inch circle. Place some of the pork mixture on five of the circles. Moisten edges. Top with remaining biscuit circles. Crimp edges to seal.

Stir together egg yolk, water and food coloring to make egg-wash paint, if desired. Using a clean paintbrush, paint desired designs on biscuit "flying saucers." Place on baking sheet. Bake 11 to 13 minutes or until golden.

Makes 5 servings

Vegetable Martians

    10 cherry tomatoes, baby pattypan squash or combination
    5 to 10 thin slices cucumber or zucchini
    ¼ teaspoon reduced-fat soft cream cheese or mustard
    5 to 8 currants, cut into halves
    10 chow mein noodles

Use wooden picks to skewer together cherry tomatoes or baby squash and cucumber or zucchini slices to from martian bodies. Use cream cheese or mustard to make eyes or to attach currants for eyes and mouths. Press 2 chow mein noodles into tops of each martian for antennae. Remove wooden picks before serving.

Makes 5 martians

Barbecue Flying Saucer with Vegetable Martians

Spicy Quick and Easy Chili

Prep and Cook Time: 15 minutes

1 pound ground beef
1 large clove garlic, minced
1 can (15¼ ounces) DEL MONTE® Whole Kernel Golden Sweet
    Corn, drained
1 can (16 ounces) kidney beans, drained
1½ cups salsa, mild, medium or hot
1 can (4 ounces) diced green chiles, undrained

1. Brown meat with garlic in large saucepan; drain.

2. Add remaining ingredients. Simmer, uncovered, 10 minutes, stirring occasionally. Sprinkle with chopped green onions, if desired.

Makes 4 servings

Spicy Quick and Easy Chili

Kids' Taco-Mac

1 pound ground beef
1 package (1.0 ounces) LAWRY'S® Taco Spices & Seasonings
1 can (14½ ounces) chopped tomatoes, undrained
1½ cups water
8 ounces uncooked macaroni or small spiral pasta
½ cup sliced celery
1 egg
⅓ cup milk
1 package (8½ ounces) corn muffin mix
½ cup (2 ounces) shredded cheddar cheese

In medium skillet, brown ground beef until crumbly; drain fat. Add Taco Spices & Seasonings, tomatoes, water, macaroni and celery; mix well. Bring to a boil over medium-high heat; reduce heat to low; cover, simmer 20 minutes, stirring occasionally. Spoon meat mixture into 2½-quart casserole dish; set aside. In medium bowl, beat egg. Stir in milk. Add muffin mix; stir with fork just until muffin mix is moistened. Spoon half of the batter over meat mixture in dollops. Spoon remaining batter into 6 greased or paper-lined medium-sized muffin cups. Bake in 400°F. oven 15 to 20 minutes or until golden. *Makes 6 to 8 servings*

Serving Suggestion: Sprinkle hot baked casserole with shredded cheddar cheese before serving.

Hint: Cool Muffins completely. Wrap tightly and freeze for later use, if desired.

Veggie & Chicken Nuggets

Prep Time: 15 minutes   *Cook Time:* 5 minutes

1 bag (16 ounces) BIRDS EYE® frozen Farm Fresh Mixtures
    Broccoli, Cauliflower & Carrots
1 box (5½ ounces) seasoning & coating mix for chicken (2 packets)
¼ to ½ teaspoon garlic powder
1 pound boneless skinless chicken breast halves, cut into 1½- to
    2-inch pieces

• Preheat oven to 400°F.

• Rinse vegetables under warm water to thaw; drain.

• In small bowl, combine coating mix with garlic powder; place ½ of mixture in resealable plastic food storage bag. Add vegetables; shake until evenly coated. Place in single layer on ungreased 15×10-inch baking pan.

• Moisten chicken with water. Add remaining coating mixture and chicken to same bag; shake until evenly coated.

• Place chicken on pan with vegetables, using additional baking pan if too crowded.

• Bake 10 to 15 minutes or until chicken is no longer pink in center.

Makes 4 servings

Serving Suggestion: Serve with a green salad tossed with Italian dressing.

Dessert Station

Brownie Turtle Cookies

2 squares (1 ounce each) unsweetened baking chocolate
⅓ cup solid vegetable shortening
1 cup granulated sugar
½ teaspoon vanilla extract
2 large eggs
1¼ cups all-purpose flour
½ teaspoon baking powder
½ teaspoon salt
1 cup "M&M's"® Milk Chocolate Mini Baking Bits, divided
1 cup pecan halves
⅓ cup caramel ice cream topping
⅓ cup shredded coconut
⅓ cup finely chopped pecans

Preheat oven to 350°F. Lightly grease cookie sheets; set aside. Heat chocolate and shortening in 2-quart saucepan over low heat, stirring constantly until melted; remove from heat. Mix in sugar, vanilla and eggs. Blend in flour, baking powder and salt. Stir in ⅔ cup "M&M's"® Milk Chocolate Mini Baking Bits. For each cookie, arrange 3 pecan halves, with ends almost touching at center, on prepared cookie sheets. Drop dough by rounded teaspoonfuls onto center of each group of pecans; mound the dough slightly. Bake 8 to 10 minutes just until set. *Do not overbake.* Cool completely on wire racks. In small bowl combine ice cream topping, coconut and chopped nuts; top each cookie with about 1½ teaspoons mixture. Press remaining ⅓ cup "M&M's"® Milk Chocolate Mini Baking Bits into topping.

Makes about 2½ dozen cookies

Puzzle Cookie

¾ cup shortening
½ cup packed light brown sugar
6 tablespoons dark molasses
2 egg whites
¾ teaspoon vanilla
2¼ cups all-purpose flour
2 teaspoons ground cinnamon
¾ teaspoon baking soda
¾ teaspoon salt
¾ teaspoon ground ginger
¼ teaspoon plus ⅛ teaspoon baking powder
  Assorted colored frostings, colored sugars, colored decorator gels
    and assorted small candies

1. Beat shortening, brown sugar, molasses, egg whites and vanilla in large bowl at high speed of electric mixer until smooth.

2. Combine flour, cinnamon, baking soda, salt, ginger and baking powder in medium bowl. Add to shortening mixture; mix well. Shape dough into flat rectangle. Wrap in plastic wrap and refrigerate about 8 hours or until firm.

3. Preheat oven to 350°F. Grease 15½×10½-inch jelly-roll pan.

4. Sprinkle dough with additional flour. Place dough in center of prepared pan and roll evenly to within ½ inch of edge of pan. Cut shapes into dough using cookie cutters or free-hand, allowing at least 1 inch between each shape. Cut through dough using sharp knife, but do not remove shapes.

5. Bake 12 minutes or until edges begin to brown lightly. Remove from oven and retrace shapes with knife. Return to oven 5 to 6 minutes. Cool in pan 5 minutes. Carefully remove shapes to wire racks; cool completely.

6. Decorate shapes with frostings, sugars, decorator gels and small candies as shown in photo. Leave puzzle frame in pan. Decorate with frostings, colored sugars and gels to represent sky, clouds, grass and water, if desired. Return shapes to their respective openings to complete puzzle.

Makes 1 puzzle cookie

Sandwich Cookies

1 package (20 ounces) refrigerated cookie dough, any flavor
All-purpose flour (optional)
Any combination of colored frostings, peanut butter or assorted ice creams for filling
Colored sprinkles, chocolate-covered raisins, miniature candy-coated chocolate pieces and other assorted small candies for decoration

1. Preheat oven to 350°F. Grease cookie sheets.

2. Remove dough from wrapper according to package directions. Cut dough into 4 equal sections. Reserve 1 section; refrigerate remaining 3 sections.

3. Roll reserved dough to ¼-inch thickness. Sprinkle with flour to minimize sticking, if necessary.

4. Cut out cookies using ¾-inch round or fluted cookie cutter. Transfer cookies to prepared cookie sheets, placing about 2 inches apart. Repeat steps with remaining dough.

5. Bake 8 to 11 minutes or until edges are lightly browned. Remove to wire racks; cool completely.

6. To make sandwich, spread about 1 tablespoon desired filling on flat side of 1 cookie to within ¼ inch of edge. Top with second cookie, pressing gently. Roll side of sandwich in desired decorations. Repeat with remaining cookies.   *Makes about 20 to 24 sandwich cookies*

Tip: Be creative—make sandwich cookies using 2 or more flavors of refrigerated cookie dough. Mix and match to see how many flavor combinations you can come up with.

Clown-Around Cones

  4 waffle cones
½ cup "M&M's"® Chocolate Mini Baking Bits, divided
    Prepared decorator icing
½ cup hot fudge ice cream topping, divided
  4 cups any flavor ice cream, softened
  1 (1.5- to 2-ounce) chocolate candy bar, chopped
¼ cup caramel ice cream topping

Decorate cones as desired with "M&M's"® Chocolate Mini Baking Bits, using decorator icing to attach; let set. For each cone, place 1 tablespoon hot fudge topping in bottom of cone. Sprinkle with 1 teaspoon "M&M's"® Chocolate Mini Baking Bits. Layer with ¼ cup ice cream; sprinkle with ¼ of candy bar. Layer with ¼ cup ice cream; sprinkle with 1 teaspoon "M&M's"® Chocolate Mini Baking Bits. Top with 1 tablespoon caramel topping and remaining ½ cup ice cream. Wrap in plastic wrap and freeze until ready to serve. Just before serving, top each ice cream cone with 1 tablespoon hot fudge topping; sprinkle with remaining "M&M's"® Chocolate Mini Baking Bits. Serve immediately. *Makes 4 servings*

Gingerbread Squares

　　3 tablespoons margarine, softened
　　2 tablespoons light brown sugar
　　¼ cup molasses
　　1 egg white
　1¼ cups all-purpose flour
　　½ teaspoon ground ginger
　　½ teaspoon ground cinnamon
　　½ teaspoon baking soda
　　¼ teaspoon salt
　　1 cup sweetened applesauce
　　　Decorations: tube frostings, colored sugars, red hot cinnamon
　　　　candies or other small candies (optional)

1. Preheat oven to 350°F. Spray 8-inch square baking pan with nonstick cooking spray; set aside.

2. Beat margarine and sugar with wooden spoon in medium bowl until well blended. Beat in molasses and egg white.

3. Combine dry ingredients in small bowl; mix well. Add to margarine mixture alternately with applesauce, mixing well after each addition. Transfer batter to prepared pan.

4. Bake 25 to 30 minutes or until wooden pick inserted in center comes out clean. Cool completely on wire rack. Cut into squares. Frost and decorate, if desired.

Makes 9 servings

The Thousand Legged Worm

**1 package (20 ounces) refrigerated sugar cookie dough
2 containers (16 ounces each) chocolate frosting
  Black licorice strings, cut into 3-inch pieces
1 marshmallow and coconut covered chocolate snack cake
  Miniature round butter cookies and assorted chewy candies**

1. Preheat oven to 350°F. Grease cookie sheets.

2. Remove dough from wrapper according to package directions.

3. Cut dough into 30 (½-inch) slices. Place 2 inches apart on prepared cookie sheets.

4. Bake 8 to 10 minutes or until edges are lightly browned. Cool completely on wire racks.

5. Spread underside of 1 cookie with 1 tablespoon frosting. Top with another cookie, pressing gently. Set aside.

6. Spread underside of another cookie with frosting, insert 1 piece of licorice into frosting on each side of cookie and attach to reserved sandwich cookie with frosting.

7. Repeat until 6 cookies are sandwiched together with frosting and licorice.

8. Place cookie stack on its side on serving platter. Repeat with remaining cookies, frosting and licorice.

9. Attach snack cake to 1 end of worm using frosting.

1. Decorate with cookies and assorted candies to resemble face.

Makes 1 worm (3 dozen cookies)

Tip: To make this party worm into a cute birthday worm, insert birthday candles into the frosting used to hold the cookies together. It's sure to be the hit of the party.

Berry Surprise Cupcakes

1 package DUNCAN HINES® Moist Deluxe® White Cake Mix
3 egg whites
1⅓ cups water
2 tablespoons vegetable oil
3 sheets (0.5 ounce each) strawberry chewy fruit snacks
1 container DUNCAN HINES® Vanilla Frosting
2 pouches (0.9 ounce each) chewy fruit snack shapes, for garnish (optional)

1. Preheat oven to 350°F. Place 24 (2½-inch) paper liners in muffin cups.

2. Combine cake mix, egg whites, water and oil in large bowl. Beat at low speed with electric mixer until moistened. Beat at medium speed 2 minutes. Fill each liner half full with batter.

3. Cut three fruit snack sheets into 9 equal pieces. (You will have 3 extra squares.) Place each fruit snack piece on top of batter in each cup. Pour remaining batter equally over each. Bake at 350°F 18 to 23 minutes or until toothpick inserted in center comes out clean. Cool in pans 5 minutes. Remove to cooling racks. Cool completely. Frost cupcakes with Vanilla frosting. Decorate with fruit snack shapes, if desired.

Makes 12 to 16 servings

Tip: To make a Berry Surprise Cake, prepare cake following package directions. Pour half the batter into prepared 13×9×2-inch pan. Place 4 fruit snack sheets evenly on top. Pour remaining batter over all. Bake and cool as directed on package. Frost and decorate as described above.

Candy Corn Cookies

Butter Cookie Dough (recipe follows)
Cookie Glaze (recipe follows)
Yellow and orange food colors

1. Prepare Butter Cookie Dough.

2. Preheat oven to 350°F. Roll dough on floured surface to ¼-inch thickness. Cut out 3-inch candy corn shapes from dough. Place cutouts on ungreased cookie sheets.

3. Bake 8 to 10 minutes or until edges are lightly browned. Remove to wire racks to cool completely. Prepare Cookie Glaze.

4. Place racks over waxed-paper-lined baking sheets. Divide Cookie Glaze into thirds; place in separate small bowls. Color ⅓ glaze with yellow food color and ⅓ with orange food color. Leave remaining glaze white. Spoon glazes over cookies to resemble candy corn as shown in photo. Let stand until glaze is set.

Makes about 2 dozen cookies

Cookie Glaze: Combine 4 cups powdered sugar and 4 tablespoons milk in small bowl. Add 1 to 2 tablespoons more milk as needed to make medium-thick, pourable glaze.

Bat Cookies: Omit yellow and orange food colors. Prepare recipe as directed except use bat cookie cutter to cut out dough. Bake as directed. Color glaze with black paste food color; spoon over cookies. Decorate with assorted candies as shown in photo.

Butter Cookie Dough

¾ cup butter, softened
¼ cup granulated sugar
¼ cup packed light brown sugar
1 egg yolk
1¾ cups all-purpose flour
¾ teaspoon baking powder
⅛ teaspoon salt

1. Combine butter, granulated sugar, brown sugar and egg yolk in medium bowl. Add flour, baking powder and salt; mix well.

2. Cover; refrigerate about 4 hours or until firm.

Bottom to top: Candy Corn Cookies, Bat Cookies

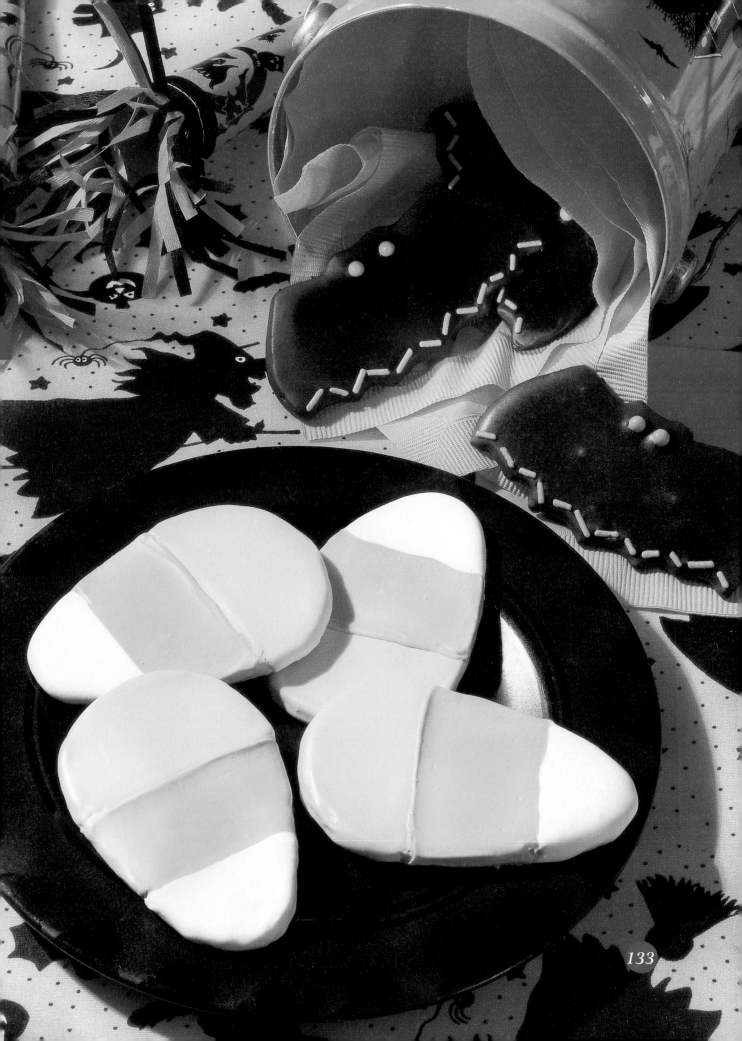

Hot Dog Cookies

Butter Cookie Dough (recipe page 132)
Liquid food colors
Sesame seeds
**Shredded coconut, red and green decorator gels, frosting and
   gummy candies**

1. Prepare Butter Cookie Dough. Cover; refrigerate 4 hours or until firm. Grease cookie sheets.

2. Reserve ⅓ of dough to make "hot dogs." Refrigerate remaining dough. Mix food colors in small bowl to get reddish-brown color following chart on back of food color box. Mix color throughout reserved dough.

3. Divide colored dough into 6 equal sections. Roll each section into thin log shape. Round edges; set aside.

4. To make "buns," divide remaining dough into 6 equal sections. Roll sections into thick logs. Make very deep indentation the length of logs in centers; smooth edges to create buns. Dip sides of buns in sesame seeds. Place 3 inches apart on prepared cookie sheets. Place hot dogs inside buns. Freeze 20 minutes.

5. Preheat oven to 350°F. Bake 17 to 20 minutes or until bun edges are light golden brown. Cool completely on cookie sheets.

6. Top hot dogs with green-tinted shredded coconut for "relish," white coconut for "onions," red decorator gel for "ketchup" and yellow-tinted frosting or whipped topping for "mustard."   *Makes 6 hot dog cookies*

Tip: To pipe gels and frosting onto Hot Dog Cookies, you can use a resealable plastic sandwich bag as a substitute for a pastry bag. Fold the top of the bag down to form a cuff and use a spatula to fill bag half full with gel or frosting. Unfold top of bag and twist down against the filling. Snip a tiny tip off one corner of bag. Hold top of bag tightly and squeeze the filling through the opening.

Kids' Cookie Dough

1 cup butter, softened
2 teaspoons vanilla
½ cup powdered sugar
2¼ cups all-purpose flour
¼ teaspoon salt
   Assorted colored glazes, frostings, sugars and small candies

1. Preheat oven to 350°F. Grease cookie sheets.

2. Beat butter and vanilla in large bowl at high speed of electric mixer until fluffy. Add sugar and beat at medium speed until blended. Combine flour and salt in small bowl. Gradually add to butter mixture.

3. Divide dough into 10 equal sections. Form shapes directly on prepared cookie sheets according to photo, or as desired, for each section.

4. Bake 15 to 18 minutes or until edges are lightly browned. Cool completely on cookie sheets.

5. Decorate cookies with glazes, frostings, sugars and small candies as desired.

Makes 10 (4-inch) cookies

Firecrackers

5 cups BAKER'S® ANGEL FLAKE® Coconut
   Blue food coloring
24 baked cupcakes, cooled
1 tub (12 ounces) COOL WHIP® Whipped Topping, thawed
   Red decorating gel
   Red string licorice

TINT coconut using blue food coloring.

TRIM any "lips" off top edges of cupcakes. Using small amount of whipped topping, attach bottoms of 2 cupcakes together. Repeat with remaining cupcakes. Stand attached cupcakes on 1 end on serving plate or tray.

FROST with remaining whipped topping. Press coconut onto sides.

DRAW a star on top of each firecracker with decorating gel. Insert pieces of licorice for fuses. Store cakes in refrigerator.

Makes 12 Firecrackers

Cookie Canvases

1 package (20 ounces) refrigerated cookie dough, any flavor
All-purpose flour (optional)
Cookie Glaze (recipe follows)
Assorted liquid food colors

Supplies

1 (3½-inch) square cardboard template
1 (2½×4½-inch) rectangular cardboard template
Small, clean craft paintbrushes

1. Preheat oven to 350°F. Grease cookie sheets.

2. Remove dough from wrapper according to package directions. Cut dough in half. Wrap half of dough in plastic wrap and refrigerate.

3. Roll remaining dough on floured surface to ¼-inch thickness. Sprinkle with flour to minimize sticking, if necessary. Cut out cookie shapes using cardboard templates as guides. Place cookies 2 inches apart on prepared cookie sheets. Repeat steps with remaining dough.

4. Bake 8 to 10 minutes or until edges are lightly browned. Remove from oven and straighten cookie edges with spatula. Cool cookies completely on cookie sheets. Prepare Cookie Glaze.

5. Place cookies on wire racks set over waxed paper. Drizzle Cookie Glaze over cookies. Let stand at room temperature 40 minutes or until glaze is set. Place food colors in small bowls. Using small, clean craft paintbrushes, decorate cookies with food colors by "painting" designs such as rainbows, flowers and animals.

Makes 8 to 10 cookie canvases

Cookie Glaze: Combine 4 cups powdered sugar and 4 tablespoons milk in a small bowl. Stir; add 1 to 2 tablespoons more milk as needed to make a medium-thick, pourable glaze.

Cookie Canvases

Snowman Cupcakes

1 package (18.5 ounces) yellow or white cake mix plus ingredients
    to prepare mix
2 containers (16 ounces each) vanilla frosting
4 cups flaked coconut
15 large marshmallows
15 miniature chocolate covered peanut butter cups, unwrapped
    Small red candies and pretzel sticks for decoration
    Green and red decorating gel

Preheat oven to 350°F. Line 15 regular-size (2½-inch) muffin pan cups and
15 small (about 1-inch) muffin pan cups with paper muffin cup liners. Prepare
cake mix according to package directions. Spoon batter into muffin cups.

Bake 10 to 15 minutes for small cupcakes and 15 to 20 minutes for large
cupcakes or until cupcakes are golden and toothpick inserted into centers
comes out clean. Cool in pans on wire racks 10 minutes. Remove from pans
to racks; cool completely. Remove paper liners.

For each snowman, frost bottom and side of 1 large cupcake; coat with
coconut. Repeat with 1 small cupcake. Attach small cupcake to large
cupcake with frosting to form snowman body. Attach marshmallow to small
cupcake with frosting to form snowman head. Attach inverted peanut
butter cup to marshmallow with frosting to form snowman hat. Use
pretzels for arms and small red candies for buttons as shown in photo. Pipe
faces with decorating gel as shown. Repeat with remaining cupcakes.

Makes 15 snowmen

Chocolate Teddy Bears

1 recipe Chocolate Cookie dough (recipe follows)
   White and colored frostings, decorator gels, coarse sugars and assorted small candies

1. Prepare Chocolate Cookie Dough. Cover; refrigerate about 2 hours or until firm.

2. Preheat oven to 325°F. Grease cookie sheets. Divide dough in half. Reserve 1 half; refrigerate remaining dough.

3. Divide reserved dough into 8 equal balls. Cut 1 ball in half; roll 1 half into ball for body. Cut other half into 2 equal pieces; roll 1 piece into 4 small balls for paws.

4. Divide second piece into thirds. Roll two-thirds of dough into ball for head. Divide remaining one-third of dough in half; roll into 2 small balls for ears.

5. Place balls together to form bear directly on prepared cookie sheet. Repeat steps with remaining dough.

6. Bake 13 to 15 minutes or until set. Cool completely on cookie sheets. Decorate with frostings, gels, sugars and assorted candies as desired.

Makes 16 (4-inch) teddy bears

Chocolate Cookie Dough

1 cup butter, softened
1 cup sugar
1 egg
1 teaspoon vanilla
2 ounces semisweet chocolate, melted
2¼ cups all-purpose flour
1 teaspoon baking powder
¼ teaspoon salt

1. Beat butter and sugar in large bowl at high speed of electric mixer until fluffy. Beat in egg and vanilla. Add melted chocolate; mix well.

2. Add flour, baking powder amd salt; mix well. Cover; refrigerate about 2 hours or until firm.

Chocolate Bar Filled Chocolate Cupcakes

Chocolate Bar Filling (recipe follows)
3 cups all-purpose flour
2 cups sugar
⅔ cup HERSHEY'S Cocoa
2 teaspoons baking soda
1 teaspoon salt
2 cups water
⅔ cup vegetable oil
2 tablespoons white vinegar
2 teaspoons vanilla extract
2 HERSHEY'S Milk Chocolate Bars (7 ounces *each*), broken into
    pieces

1. Prepare Chocolate Bar Filling.

2. Heat oven to 350°F. Line muffin cups (2½ inches in diameter) with paper bake cups.

3. Stir together flour, sugar, cocoa, baking soda and salt in large bowl. Add water, oil, vinegar and vanilla; beat on medium speed of mixer 2 minutes. Fill muffin cups ⅔ full with batter. Spoon 1 level tablespoon prepared filling into center of each cupcake.

4. Bake 20 to 25 minutes or until wooden pick inserted in cake portion comes out clean. Remove from pans to wire racks. Cool completely. Top each cupcake with chocolate bar piece.   *Makes about 2½ dozen cupcakes*

Chocolate Bar Filling

1 package (8 ounces) cream cheese, softened
⅓ cup sugar
1 egg
⅛ teaspoon salt
1 HERSHEY'S Milk Chocolate Bar (7 ounces), cut into ¼-inch
    pieces

1. Beat cream cheese, sugar, egg and salt in small bowl until smooth and creamy. Stir in chocolate bar pieces.

Butterfly Cupcakes

      1 cup cold milk
      1 package (4-serving size) JELL-O® Instant Pudding & Pie Filling,
          any flavor
      1 tub (8 ounces) COOL WHIP® Whipped Topping, thawed
     24 baked cupcakes, cooled
          Multi-colored sprinkles
          Miniature flower candies
          Black or red string licorice

POUR milk into large bowl. Add pudding mix. Beat with wire whisk 1 to
2 minutes. Gently stir in whipped topping. Reserve 1 teaspoon pudding
mixture; set aside.

CUT top off each cupcake. Cut each top in half; set aside. Spoon 2 heaping
tablespoons pudding mixture on top of each cupcake. Sprinkle with multi-
colored sprinkles.

PLACE 2 cupcake top halves, cut sides together, into pudding mixture,
raising outside ends slightly to resemble butterfly wings. Lightly dip candies
into reserved pudding mixture; arrange on cupcake wings. Insert pieces of
licorice into pudding mixture to resemble antennae. Store cupcakes in
refrigerator.   *Makes 24 cupcakes*

Letters of the Alphabet

Gingerbread Cookie Dough (recipe follows)
**Colored frostings and glazes, colored sugars, sprinkles and
   assorted small candies**

1. Prepare Gingerbread Cookie Dough. Cover; refrigerate about 8 hours or until firm. Preheat oven to 350°F. Grease cookie sheets.

2. Divide dough into 4 equal sections. Reserve 1 section; cover and refrigerate remaining 3 sections. Roll reserved dough on well-floured surface to ⅛-inch thickness. Sprinkle with flour to minimize sticking, if necessary.

3. Cut out alphabet letter shapes using 2½-inch cookie cutters. Place cutouts on prepared cookie sheets. Repeat steps with remaining dough.

4. Bake 6 to 8 minutes or until edges begin to brown. Remove cookies to wire racks; cool completely.

5. Decorate cookies with frostings, glazes, colored sugars, sprinkles and assorted small candies. *Makes about 5 dozen cookies*

Tip: Encourage children to arrange letters to spell names of people they know, their favorite animals or pets, colors or even of places they like to go. A tasty way to learn the ABC's.

Gingerbread Cookie Dough

½ **cup shortening**
⅓ **cup packed light brown sugar**
¼ **cup dark molasses**
1 **egg white**
½ **teaspoon vanilla**
1½ **cups all-purpose flour**
1 **teaspoon ground cinnamon**
½ **teaspoon baking soda**
½ **teaspoon salt**
½ **teaspoon ground ginger**
¼ **teaspoon baking powder**

1. Beat shortening, brown sugar, molasses, egg white and vanilla in large bowl at high speed of electric mixer until smooth.

2. Combine flour, cinnamon, baking soda, salt, ginger and baking powder in small bowl. Add to shortening mixture; mix well. Cover; refrigerate about 8 hours or until firm.

147

Kids' Favorite Jumbo Chippers

1 cup butter, softened
¾ cup granulated sugar
¾ cup packed brown sugar
2 eggs
1 teaspoon vanilla
2¼ cups all-purpose flour
1 teaspoon baking soda
¾ teaspoon salt
1¼ cups "M&M's"® Milk Chocolate Candies
1 cup peanut butter flavored chips

Preheat oven to 375°F. Beat butter, granulated sugar and brown sugar in large bowl until light and fluffy. Beat in eggs and vanilla. Add flour, baking soda and salt. Beat until well blended. Stir in "M&M's"® Chocolate Candies and peanut butter chips. Drop by rounded tablespoonfuls 3 inches apart onto ungreased cookie sheets. Bake 10 to 12 minutes or until edges are golden brown. Let cookies stand on cookie sheets 2 minutes. Remove cookies to wire racks; cool completely.   *Makes 3 dozen cookies*

Note: For a change of pace, substitute "M&M's"® Crispy Chocolate Candies, "M&M's"® Peanut Chocolate Candies, "M&M's"® Almond Chocolate Candies, or "M&M's"® Peanut Butter Chocolate Candies for the chocolate candies.

Kids' Favorite Jumbo Chippers

Touchdown Brownie Cups

1 cup (2 sticks) butter or margarine
½ cup HERSHEY'S Cocoa or HERSHEY'S Dutch Processed Cocoa
1 cup packed light brown sugar
½ cup granulated sugar
3 eggs
1 teaspoon vanilla extract
1 cup all-purpose flour
1⅓ cup chopped pecans, divided

1. Heat oven to 350°F. Line 2½-inch muffin cups with paper or foil bake cups.

2. Place butter in large microwave-safe bowl; cover. Microwave at HIGH (100%) 1½ minutes or until melted. Add cocoa; stir until smooth. Add brown sugar and granulated sugar; stir until well blended. Add eggs and vanilla; beat well. Add flour and 1 cup pecans; stir until well blended. Fill prepared muffin cups about ¾ full with batter; sprinkle about 1 teaspoon remaining pecans over top of each.

3. Bake 20 to 25 minutes or until tops are beginning to dry and crack on top. Cool completely in cups on wire rack. *Makes about 17 cupcakes*

Touchdown Brownie Cups

PB & J Cookie Sandwiches

½ cup butter or margarine, softened
½ cup creamy peanut butter
¼ cup solid vegetable shortening
1 cup firmly packed light brown sugar
1 large egg
1 teaspoon vanilla extract
1⅔ cups all-purpose flour
1 teaspoon baking soda
½ teaspoon baking powder
1 cup "M&M's"® Milk Chocolate Mini Baking Bits
½ cup finely chopped peanuts
½ cup grape or strawberry jam

Preheat oven to 350°F. In large bowl cream butter, peanut butter, shortening and sugar until light and fluffy; beat in egg and vanilla. In medium bowl combine flour, baking soda and baking powder; blend into creamed mixture. Stir in "M&M's"® Milk Chocolate Mini Baking Bits and nuts. Drop by rounded teaspoonfuls onto ungreased cookie sheets. Bake 8 to 10 minutes or until light golden brown. Let cool 2 minutes on cookie sheets; remove to wire racks to cool completely. Just before serving, spread ½ teaspoon jam on bottom of one cookie; top with second cookie. Store in tightly covered container.   *Makes about 2 dozen sandwich cookies*

Handprints

**1 package (20 ounces) refrigerated cookie dough, any flavor
All-purpose flour (optional)
Cookie glazes, frostings, nondairy whipped topping, peanut
   butter and assorted candies**

1. Grease cookie sheets. Remove dough from wrapper according to package directions.

2. Cut dough into 4 equal sections. Reserve 1 section; refrigerate remaining 3 sections. Sprinkle reserved dough with flour to minimize sticking, if necessary.

3. Roll dough on prepared cookie sheet to 5×7-inch rectangle.

4. Place hand, palm-side down, on dough. Carefully, cut around outline of hand with knife. Remove scraps. Separate fingers as much as possible using small spatula. Pat fingers outward to lengthen slightly. Repeat steps with remaining dough.

5. Freeze dough 15 minutes. Preheat oven to 350°F.

6. Bake 7 to 13 minutes or until cookies are set and edges are golden brown. Cool completely on cookie sheets.

7. Decorate as desired.   *Makes 5 adult handprint cookies*

Tip: To get the kids involved, let them use their hands to make the handprints. Be sure that an adult is available to cut around the outline with a knife. The kids will enjoy seeing how their handprints bake into big cookies.

Little Devils

Prep Time: 20 minutes

1 package (18 ounces) carrot cake mix
½ cup solid pack pumpkin
⅓ cup vegetable oil
3 eggs
1 container (16 ounces) cream cheese frosting
   Assorted Halloween candies, jelly beans, chocolate candies
   and nuts

1. Preheat oven to 350°F. Prepare cake mix according to package directions, using water as directed on package, pumpkin, oil and eggs. Spoon batter into 18 paper-lined muffin cups. Bake 20 minutes or until toothpick inserted in centers of cupcakes comes out clean. Cool in pans on wire racks 5 minutes; remove and cool completely.

2. Frost cupcakes with frosting. Let each goblin guest decorate his own cupcake with assorted candies. *Makes 18 cupcakes*

I Think You're "Marbleous" Cupcakes

1 box (18½ ounces) pudding-in-the-mix cake mix, any flavor
1¼ cups water
3 eggs
¼ cup oil
1 container (16 ounces) vanilla frosting
1 tube (4¼ ounces) red decorating icing

Supplies
   Decorating tips to fit tube of icing

1. Preheat oven to 350°F. Grease or paper-line 24 (2½-inch) muffin cups.

2. Prepare cake mix according to package directions with water, eggs and oil. Spoon batter into prepared pans, filling each ⅔ full.

3. Bake 20 to 25 minutes or until toothpick inserted into centers comes out clean. Cool in pans 20 minutes. Remove to wire rack and cool completely.

4. Spread 1½ to 2 tablespoons frosting over each cupcake. Fit round tip onto tube of icing. Squeeze 4 to 5 dots icing over each cupcake. Swirl toothpick through icing and frosting in continuous motion to make marbleized pattern or heart shapes. *Makes about 2 dozen cupcakes*

Lollipop Sugar Cookies

1¼ cups granulated sugar
1 cup Butter Flavor CRISCO® all-vegetable shortening or 1 Butter Flavor CRISCO® Stick
2 eggs
¼ cup light corn syrup or regular pancake syrup
1 tablespoon vanilla
3 cups all-purpose flour
¾ teaspoon baking powder
½ teaspoon baking soda
½ teaspoon salt
36 flat ice cream sticks
Any of the following: miniature baking chips, raisins, red hots, nonpareils, colored sugar or nuts

1. Combine sugar and shortening in large bowl. Beat at medium speed of electric mixer until well blended. Add eggs, syrup and vanilla; beat until well blended and fluffy.

2. Combine flour, baking powder, baking soda and salt. Add gradually to creamed mixture at low speed until well blended. Wrap dough in plastic wrap. Refrigerate at least 1 hour.

3. Heat oven to 375°F. Place foil on countertop for cooling cookies.

4. Shape dough into 1½-inch balls. Push ice cream stick into center of each ball. Place balls 3 inches apart on ungreased baking sheet. Flatten balls to ½-inch thickness with bottom of greased and floured glass. Decorate as desired; press decorations gently into dough.*

5. Bake at 375°F for 8 to 10 minutes. *Do not overbake.* Cool on baking sheet 2 minutes. Remove cookies to foil to cool completely.

Makes about 3 dozen cookies

Cookies can also be painted before baking. Mix 1 egg yolk and ¼ teaspoon water. Divide into 3 small cups. Add 2 to 3 drops food color to each. Stir. Use clean water color brushes to paint designs on cookies.

Cakes for Any Occasion

Crayon Craze

1 (13×9-inch) cake
1 (14×10-inch) cake board, covered, or large platter
2 cans (16 ounces each) white frosting
4 flat-bottomed ice cream cones

1. Trim top and side of cake. Measure 4½ inches down long sides of cake; draw line across top of cake with wooden toothpick to create 9×4½-inch rectangle. Using toothpick line as guide, carefully cut halfway through cake (about 1 inch). Do *not* cut all the way through.

2. Cut cake in half horizontally from 9-inch side just to horizontal cut made at 4½-inch line. Remove 9×4½×1-inch piece of cake; reserve for another use. Round edges of 9-inch side to resemble top of crayon box. Place cake on prepared cake board.

3. Tint 1 can frosting gold. Tint 1 cup frosting green. Divide remaining frosting into 4 parts, (about ¼ cup each). Tint one part red, one yellow, one orange and one blue.

4. Frost entire cake with gold frosting. Using medium writing tip and green frosting, pipe the word CRAYONS on cake. Pipe stripes and two green triangles on bottom of box and decorative borders around box.

5. Gently cut ice cream cones in half vertically with serrated knife. Frost each cone different color (red, yellow, orange and blue). Place frosted cones on cake, just below rounded edge, to resemble crayon tips.

Makes 16 to 18 servings

Banana Split Cake

1 package DUNCAN HINES® Moist Deluxe® Banana Supreme
    Cake Mix
3 eggs
1⅓ cups water
½ cup all-purpose flour
⅓ cup vegetable oil
1 cup semi-sweet mini chocolate chips
2 to 3 bananas
1 can (16 ounces) chocolate syrup
1 container (8 ounces) frozen whipped topping, thawed
½ cup chopped walnuts
    Colored sprinkles
    Maraschino cherries with stems, for garnish

1. Preheat oven to 350°F. Grease and flour 13×9×2-inch pan.

2. Combine cake mix, eggs, water, flour and oil in large bowl. Beat at low speed with electric mixer until moistened. Beat at medium speed 2 minutes. Stir in chocolate chips. Pour into pan. Bake at 350°F 32 to 35 minutes or until toothpick inserted in center comes out clean. Cool completely.

3. Slice bananas. Cut cake into squares; top with banana slices. Drizzle with chocolate syrup. Top with whipped topping, walnuts and sprinkles. Garnish with maraschino cherries. *Makes 12 to 16 servings*

Tip: Dip bananas in diluted lemon juice to prevent darkening.

Banana Split Cake

Quick & Easy Chocolate Cake

4 bars (4 ounces) HERSHEY'S Unsweetened Baking Chocolate,
    broken into pieces
¼ cup (½ stick) butter or margarine
1⅔ cups boiling water
2⅓ cups all-purpose flour
2 cups sugar
½ cup dairy sour cream
2 eggs
2 teaspoons baking soda
1 teaspoon salt
1 teaspoon vanilla extract

1. Heat oven to 350°F. Grease and flour 13×9×2-inch baking pan.

2. Combine chocolate, butter and water in large bowl; with spoon, stir until chocolate is melted and mixture is smooth. Add flour, sugar, sour cream, eggs, baking soda, salt and vanilla; beat on low speed of mixer until smooth. Pour batter into prepared pan.

3. Bake 35 to 40 minutes or until wooden pick inserted in center comes out clean. Cool completely in pan on wire rack. Frost as desired.

Makes 12 to 15 servings

Chocolate Spider Web Cake

1⅔ cups all-purpose flour
1½ cups sugar
 ½ cup HERSHEY'S Cocoa
1½ teaspoons baking soda
 1 teaspoon salt
 ½ teaspoon baking powder
 2 eggs
1½ cups buttermilk or sour milk*
 ½ cup shortening (do *not* use butter, margarine, spread or oil)
 1 teaspoon vanilla extract
 One-Bowl Buttercream Frosting (recipe page 164)
 Spider Web (recipe page 164)

*To sour milk: Use 4½ teaspoons white vinegar plus milk to equal 1½ cups.

1. Heat oven to 350°F. Thoroughly grease and flour two 9-inch round baking pans.

2. Combine dry ingredients in large bowl; add eggs, buttermilk, shortening and vanilla. Beat on low speed of mixer 1 minute, scraping bowl constantly. Beat on high speed 3 minutes, scraping bowl occasionally. Pour batter into prepared pans.

3. Bake 30 to 35 minutes or until wooden pick inserted in centers comes out clean. Cool 10 minutes; remove from pans to wire racks. Cool completely.

4. Frost with One-Bowl Buttercream Frosting. Immediately pipe or drizzle Spider Web in 4 or 5 circles on top of cake. Using a knife or wooden pick, immediately draw 8 to 10 lines from center to edges of cake at regular intervals to form web. Garnish with "spider," using cookie, licorice and other candies.

Makes 12 servings

Continued on page 164

Continued from page 163

One-Bowl Buttercream Frosting

6 tablespoons butter or margarine, softened
2⅔ cups powdered sugar
½ cup HERSHEY'S Cocoa
4 to 6 tablespoons milk
1 teaspoon vanilla extract

Beat butter; add powdered sugar and cocoa alternately with milk, beating
to spreading consistency. Stir in vanilla. *Makes about 2 cups frosting*

Spider Web: Place ½ cup HERSHEY'S Premier White Chips and
½ teaspoon shortening (do not use butter, margarine, spread or oil) in small
heavy seal-top plastic bag. Microwave at HIGH (100%) 45 seconds.
Squeeze gently. If necessary, microwave an additional 10 to 15 seconds;
squeeze until chips are melted. With scissors, make small diagonal cut in
bottom corner of bag; squeeze mixture onto cake as directed.

Chocolate Spider Web Cake

Double Dip Ice Cream Cone Cakes

1 package (2-layer size) cake mix, any flavor
4 squares BAKER'S® Semi-Sweet Chocolate
¼ cup milk
1 tub (8 ounces) COOL WHIP® Whipped Topping, thawed
    Assorted small candies
    Multicolored sprinkles
    Maraschino cherries

HEAT oven to 350°F.

PREPARE cake mix as directed on package. Divide batter evenly between greased and floured 8-inch round and 8-inch square baking pans. Bake as directed on package. Cool 10 minutes; remove from pans. Cool completely on wire racks.

CUT cakes as shown in Diagram 1. Assemble pieces on large serving tray as shown in Diagram 2.

MICROWAVE chocolate and milk in medium microwavable bowl on HIGH 2 minutes or until chocolate is almost melted. Stir until chocolate is completely melted. Cool 20 minutes or until room temperature. Gently stir 1½ cups whipped topping into chocolate with wire whisk until blended.

FROST "cones" with chocolate whipped topping mixture; decorate with candies, if desired. Frost "ice cream" with remaining whipped topping; decorate with sprinkles.

REFRIGERATE until ready to serve. Top with cherries just before serving.

Makes 12 to 14 servings

Double Dip Ice Cream Cone Cake

Merry-Go-Round Cake

Prep Time: 30 minutes   *Baking Time:* 50 minutes

1 package (6-serving size) JELL-O® Instant Pudding and Pie
    Filling, Vanilla Flavor
1 package (2-layer size) yellow cake mix
4 eggs
1 cup water
¼ cup vegetable oil
⅓ cup BAKER'S® Semi-Sweet Real Chocolate Chunks, melted
⅔ cup cold milk
    Sprinkles (optional)
    Paper carousel roof (directions follow)
3 plastic straws
6 animal crackers

RESERVE ⅓ cup pudding mix. Combine cake mix, remaining pudding mix, eggs, water and oil in large bowl. Beat at low speed of electric mixer just to moisten, scraping sides of bowl often. Beat at medium speed 4 minutes. Pour ½ of the batter into greased and floured 10-inch fluted tube pan. Mix chocolate into remaining batter. Spoon over batter in pan; cut through with spatula in zigzag pattern to marbleize. Bake at 350°F for 50 minutes or until cake tester inserted in center comes out clean. Cool in pan 15 minutes. Remove from pan; finish cooling on rack.

BEAT reserved pudding mix and milk in small bowl until smooth. Spoon over top of cake to glaze. Garnish with sprinkles, if desired.

CUT 10- to 12-inch circle from colored paper; scallop edges, if desired. Make 1 slit to center. Overlap cut edges to form carousel roof; secure with tape. Cut straws in half; arrange on cake with animal crackers. Top with roof.

Makes 12 servings

Kids' Confetti Cake

Cake

>   1 package DUNCAN HINES® Moist Deluxe® Classic Yellow
>   Cake Mix
>   1 package (4-serving size) vanilla instant pudding and pie
>   filling mix
>   4 eggs
>   1 cup water
>   ½ cup vegetable oil
>   1 cup semi-sweet mini chocolate chips

Topping

>   1 cup colored miniature marshmallows
>   ⅔ cup DUNCAN HINES® Creamy Home-Style Chocolate Frosting
>   2 tablespoons semi-sweet mini chocolate chips

1. Preheat oven to 350°F. Grease and flour 13×9×2-inch baking pan.

2. For cake, combine cake mix, pudding mix, eggs, water and oil in large bowl. Beat at medium speed with electric mixer 2 minutes. Stir in 1 cup chocolate chips. Pour into pan. Bake 40 to 45 minutes or until toothpick inserted in center comes out clean.

3. For topping, immediately arrange marshmallows evenly over hot cake. Place frosting in microwave-safe bowl. Microwave at HIGH (100% power) 25 to 30 seconds. Stir until smooth. Drizzle evenly over marshmallows and cake. Sprinkle with 2 tablespoons chocolate chips. Cool completely.

Makes 12 to 16 servings

Jack-O'-Lantern

2 (10-inch) Bundt cakes
   Buttercream Frosting (recipe page 173)
   Orange, green and brown paste food colors
   Base Frosting (recipe page 173, optional)
   Candy corn

Supplies
   2 (10-inch) round cake boards, stacked and covered, or large plate
   1 (6-ounce) paper cup or ice cream wafer cone
   Pastry bag and medium writing tip

1. Prepare 2 recipes Buttercream Frosting. Tint 4½ cups frosting orange, ½ cup dark green and ¼ cup dark brown. To tint frosting, add small amount of desired paste color with toothpick; stir well. Slowly add more color until frosting is desired shade.

2. Trim flat sides of cakes. Place one cake on prepared cake board, flat-side up. Frost top of cake with some of the orange frosting. Place second cake, flat-side down, over frosting.

3. Frost entire cake with Base Frosting to seal in crumbs. Frost again with orange frosting.

4. Hold cup over fingers of one hand. Using other hand, frost cup with green frosting. Place upside-down in center of cake to form stem. Touch up frosting, if necessary.

5. Using writing tip and brown frosting, pipe eyes and mouth. Arrange candy corn for teeth as shown in photo. Before serving, remove stem. Slice and serve top cake first, then bottom.   *Makes 36 to 40 servings*

Tip: A fall birthday is the perfect opportunity for a party with a Halloween theme. Create scary decorations like spiderwebs and bats hanging from the ceiling and perhaps a coffin or graveyard scene. Turn down the lights and play a tape of scary sounds to add to the spooky atmosphere. Costumes are, of course, required but you may want to make masks as part of the party. Provide a plain mask for each child and supply plenty of paints, markers, construction paper, crepe paper, fabric, yarn and glitter. Stickers are also an easy way to decorate. Awards can be given for the scariest, prettiest or most creative—just be sure every child wins something.

Base Frosting

3 cups powdered sugar, sifted
½ cup vegetable shortening
¼ cup milk
½ teaspoon vanilla
   Additional milk

Combine sugar, shortening, ¼ cup milk and vanilla in large bowl. Beat until smooth. Add more milk, 1 teaspoon at a time, until frosting is a thin consistency. Use frosting immediately. *Makes about 2 cups*

Buttercream Frosting

6 cups powdered sugar, sifted and divided
¾ cup butter or margarine, softened
¼ cup shortening
6 to 8 tablespoons milk, divided
1 teaspoon vanilla

Combine 3 cups powdered sugar, butter, shortening, 4 tablespoons milk and vanilla in large bowl. Beat until smooth. Add remaining powdered sugar; beat until light and fluffy, adding more milk, 1 tablespoon at a time, as needed for good spreading consistency. *Makes about 3½ cups*

Treasure Chest

1 package (12 ounces) pound cake
1 tub (8 ounces) COOL WHIP® Whipped Topping, thawed
  Assorted "jewels," such as: fruit chews, candy necklaces, cubed
    prepared JELL-O® Brand Gelatin, raspberries, gumdrops or
    other small candies
1 pretzel rod, cut into 3 pieces
  Miniature candy-coated semi-sweet chocolate candies
  Black licorice
2 pretzels

CUT ½-inch-horizontal slice off top of cake; set slice aside. Carefully hollow out center of cake, leaving ½-inch shell on bottom and sides; reserve removed cake for snacking or other use. Spoon 1 cup of the whipped topping into cake shell. Frost sides with 1½ cups whipped topping.

REFRIGERATE until ready to serve. Just before serving, place assorted "jewels" over whipped topping in cake shell. Angle reserved cake slice over jewels using pretzel rod pieces to resemble an open chest lid. Frost slice with remaining whipped topping. Decorate with miniature candy-coated semi-sweet chocolate candies and licorice. Add remaining pretzels to ends of chest for handles.   *Makes 8 servings*

Heavenly Angel Cake

Ingredients

1 package (2-layer size) white cake mix plus ingredients to prepare
   mix
1 container (16 ounces) vanilla frosting
   Yellow and red food colors
   White chocolate bar
   Decorations: white chocolate chips; pastel-colored candy-coated
      chocolate candies; red string licorice; yogurt- or white-
      chocolate-covered mini pretzels; yellow, pink and blue colored
      sugars

Supplies

1 large tray or (17×12-inch) cake board, covered

1. Preheat oven to 350°F. Grease and flour two 9-inch round baking pans.

2. Prepare cake mix according to package directions. Divide evenly into prepared cake pans.

3. Bake 30 to 35 minutes or until wooden toothpick inserted into centers comes out clean. Cool in pans on wire racks 10 minutes. Remove from pans to racks; cool completely.

4. Using diagrams 1 and 2 as guides, cut out cake pieces (make pattern out of waxed paper to use as templates). Arrange pieces on tray as shown in diagram 3, connecting pieces with small amount of frosting.

5. Color about ½ of the frosting yellow with a few drops yellow food color; color remaining frosting pink with a few drops red food color. Spread body and head of angel with pink frosting; frost wings and halo with yellow frosting.

6. Soften bar of white chocolate slightly by holding in hands. Using vegetable peeler, make curls from chocolate bar; sprinkle over body of angel. Decorate with remaining ingredients as shown in photo.

Makes 10 servings

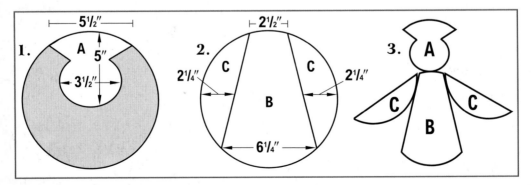

Enchanted Castle

5½ cups cake batter, divided
1 (15×15-inch) cake board, covered, or large platter
2 cans (16 ounces each) white frosting
4 sugar ice cream cones
50 chocolate-covered wafer cookies
9 square dark chocolate mints
Assorted candies, decors and fruit rollups

1. Preheat oven to 350°F. Grease and flour 9-inch square cake pan and medium muffin pan. Pour 3½ cups cake batter into cake pan; pour remaining cake batter into muffin pan (¼ cup batter per muffin cup). Bake cake in pan 35 to 45 minutes and cupcakes about 20 minutes or until toothpick inserted into centers comes out clean. Cool 15 minutes in pans. Loosen edges; invert onto wire racks and cool completely.

2. Trim top and sides of square cake and tops of four cupcakes. (Reserve remaining cupcakes for another use.) Place cake on prepared cake board. Place one cupcake upside down on each corner of cake, attaching with small amount of frosting.

3. Tint 1 can frosting pink. Divide second can of frosting in half; tint half yellow and half purple.

4. Frost entire cake and cupcakes with pink frosting. Frost ice cream cones with yellow frosting.

5. Place frosted cones on top of cupcakes. Using medium writing tip and purple frosting, pipe decorative lines around tops and bottoms of cones, cupcakes and edges of square cake.

6. Place chocolate wafer cookies around sides of cake, alternating whole cookies with cookies cut down by one fourth to create castle wall. Decorate castle with assorted candies, cookies, decors and fruit rollups cut into flag shapes.

Makes 14 to 16 servings

Enchanted Castle

Touchdown!

1 (13×9-inch) cake
1 (19×13-inch) cake board, cut in half crosswise and covered, or
    large platter
2 cups prepared white frosting
    Assorted color decorator gels
1 square (2 ounces) almond bark
2 pretzel rods
4 thin pretzel sticks
    Small bear-shaped graham cookies

1. Trim top and sides of cake; place on prepared cake board.

2. Tint frosting medium green.

3. Frost entire cake with green frosting. Pipe field lines with white decorator gel.

4. Melt almond bark in tall glass according to package directions. Break off one quarter of each pretzel rod; discard shorter pieces. Break 2 pretzel sticks in half. Dip pretzels in melted almond bark, turning to coat completely and tapping off excess. Using pretzel rods for support posts, pretzel sticks for crossbars and pretzel stick halves for uprights, arrange pretzels in two goalpost formations on waxed paper; let stand until completely dry. When dry, carefully peel waxed paper from goalposts; place on each end of cake.

5. Meanwhile, decorate bear-shaped cookies with decorator gels; position cookies throughout field as desired. *Makes 16 to 20 servings*

Radio Fun

Cake & Frostings
1 (9-inch) square cake
1 cup Base Frosting (recipe page 173), if desired
3 cups Buttercream Frosting (recipe page 173)*

Decorations & Equipment
Pink and black licorice pieces
2 yellow candy discs
1 orange flat gumdrop
1 (19×13-inch) cake board, cut into 10×10-inch square and covered
Icing comb
Pastry bags, small writing tip and basketweave tip

Color 2 cups frosting green and 1 cup yellow.

1. Trim top and edges of cake. Cut as shown in diagram.

2. Place cake on prepared cake board.

3. Frost entire cake with Base Frosting to seal in crumbs.

4. Frost as shown in photo, reserving small portion of each color for piping. While frosting is soft, use icing comb as shown in photo below to make design for speaker.**

5. Using flat side of basketweave tip and reserved yellow frosting, pipe two vertical lines, one at end of speaker section and another 2 inches from the first line.

6. Using writing tip and reserved green frosting, pipe accents on handle as shown.

7. Position candies as shown.

Makes 10 to 14 servings

**Design on speaker can also be made with fork.*

Dreidel Cake

1 package (2-layer size) cake mix, any flavor
1¼ cups water
3 eggs
¾ cup sliced or slivered almonds, toasted* and finely ground
¼ cup vegetable oil
½ teaspoon almond extract
1½ containers (16 ounces each) cream cheese frosting
Yellow and blue food colors

Supplies
1 large tray or (15×10-inch) cake board, covered
Pastry bag and medium star tip

To toast almonds, place in single layer on baking sheet. Bake at 350°F 7 to 10 minutes or until golden brown, stirring occasionally. Cool completely.

1. Preheat oven to 350°F. Grease and flour 13×9-inch baking pan.

2. Combine cake mix, water, eggs, almonds, oil and extract in medium bowl. Beat at low speed of electric mixer until blended. Beat at medium speed 2 minutes. Pour batter into prepared pan. Bake 35 to 40 minutes until wooden toothpick inserted into center comes out clean. Cool in pan on wire rack 10 minutes. Remove from pan; cool completely on rack.

3. If cake top is rounded, trim horizontally with long serrated knife. Cut cake as shown in diagram 1. Position cake pieces on tray as shown in diagram 2, connecting pieces with small amount of frosting. Frost center of cake with about ½ cup white frosting as shown in photo.

4. Tint about ¾ cup frosting yellow. To tint frosting, add small amount of desired food color; stir well. Slowly add more color until frosting is desired shade. Spread onto top and sides of cake as shown in photo.

5. Using diagram 3 as guide, cut out letter from waxed paper; position on cake as shown in photo. Trace around pattern with wooden toothpick; remove pattern. Tint remaining frosting blue. Spoon frosting into pastry bag fitted with star tip. Pipe stars to fill in symbol and pipe around top edge of cake as shown in photo. *Makes 12 servings*

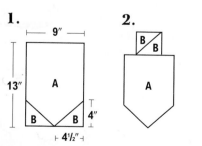

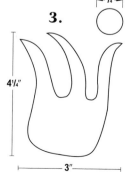

Dreidel Cake

Tropical Snack Cake

1 ½ cups all-purpose flour
 1 cup QUAKER® Oats (quick or old fashioned, uncooked)
 ¼ cup granulated sugar *or* 2 tablespoons fructose
 2 teaspoons baking powder
 ½ teaspoon baking soda
 ¼ teaspoon salt (optional)
 1 can (8 ounces) crushed pineapple in juice, undrained
 ½ cup fat-free milk
 ⅓ cup mashed ripe banana
 ¼ cup egg substitute *or* 2 egg whites
 2 tablespoons vegetable oil
 2 teaspoons vanilla

Heat oven to 350°F. Grease and flour 8×8-inch square baking pan.
Combine first 6 ingredients; mix well. Set aside. Blend pineapple, milk,
banana, egg substitute, oil and vanilla until mixed thoroughly. Add to dry
ingredients, mixing just until moistened. Pour into prepared pan. Bake
45 to 50 minutes or until golden brown and wooden pick inserted in center
comes out clean. Cool slightly before serving.   *Makes 12 servings*

Acknowledgments

Birds Eye®

ConAgra Foods®ConAgra Foods Retail Products Company - Grocery Foods Group

Del Monte Corporation

Duncan Hines® and Moist Deluxe® are registered trademarks of Aurora Foods Inc.

Equal® sweetener

Hershey Foods Corporation

Hillshire Farm®

Kraft Foods Holdings

Lawry's® Foods, Inc.

© Mars, Incorporated 2002

Mauna La'i® is a registered trademark of Mott's, Inc.

Mr & Mrs T® is a registered trademark of Mott's, Inc.

National Honey Board

Nestlé USA

The Quaker® Oatmeal Kitchens

Reckitt Benckiser

The J.M. Smucker Company

Southeast United Dairy Industry Association, Inc.

StarKist® Seafood Company

Unilever Bestfoods North America

Index

METRIC CONVERSION CHART

VOLUME MEASUREMENTS (dry)

$1/8$ teaspoon = 0.5 mL
$1/4$ teaspoon = 1 mL
$1/2$ teaspoon = 2 mL
$3/4$ teaspoon = 4 mL
1 teaspoon = 5 mL
1 tablespoon = 15 mL
2 tablespoons = 30 mL
$1/4$ cup = 60 mL
$1/3$ cup = 75 mL
$1/2$ cup = 125 mL
$2/3$ cup = 150 mL
$3/4$ cup = 175 mL
1 cup = 250 mL
2 cups = 1 pint = 500 mL
3 cups = 750 mL
4 cups = 1 quart = 1 L

VOLUME MEASUREMENTS (fluid)

1 fluid ounce (2 tablespoons) = 30 mL
4 fluid ounces ($1/2$ cup) = 125 mL
8 fluid ounces (1 cup) = 250 mL
12 fluid ounces ($1 1/2$ cups) = 375 mL
16 fluid ounces (2 cups) = 500 mL

WEIGHTS (mass)

$1/2$ ounce = 15 g
1 ounce = 30 g
3 ounces = 90 g
4 ounces = 120 g
8 ounces = 225 g
10 ounces = 285 g
12 ounces = 360 g
16 ounces = 1 pound = 450 g

DIMENSIONS

$1/16$ inch = 2 mm
$1/8$ inch = 3 mm
$1/4$ inch = 6 mm
$1/2$ inch = 1.5 cm
$3/4$ inch = 2 cm
1 inch = 2.5 cm

OVEN TEMPERATURES

250°F = 120°C
275°F = 140°C
300°F = 150°C
325°F = 160°C
350°F = 180°C
375°F = 190°C
400°F = 200°C
425°F = 220°C
450°F = 230°C

BAKING PAN SIZES

Utensil	Size in Inches/Quarts	Metric Volume	Size in Centimeters
Baking or Cake Pan (square or rectangular)	8×8×2	2 L	20×20×5
	9×9×2	2.5 L	23×23×5
	12×8×2	3 L	30×20×5
	13×9×2	3.5 L	33×23×5
Loaf Pan	8×4×3	1.5 L	20×10×7
	9×5×3	2 L	23×13×7
Round Layer Cake Pan	8×1½	1.2 L	20×4
	9×1½	1.5 L	23×4
Pie Plate	8×1¼	750 mL	20×3
	9×1¼	1 L	23×3
Baking Dish or Casserole	1 quart	1 L	—
	1½ quart	1.5 L	—
	2 quart	2 L	—